THE RAPTURE
OF THE CHURCH

DR SHAUN MARLER

The Rapture of the Church
by Dr. Shaun Marler

Published by:
World Harvest Ministries, PO Box 90, Bald Hills, Qld, 4036, Australia
www.whm.org.au

This book or parts thereof may not be reproduced in any form, stored in a retrieval system, or transmitted in any form, by any means - electronic, mechanical, photocopy, recording or otherwise - without prior written permission of the author or publisher, except as provided by Australian copyright law.

All scriptural references are taken from the King James Bible unless otherwise stated.

Cover Design by Sarah Freeman

Photo by psychoshadowmaker / www.123rf.com/profile_psychoshadowmaker

Copyright © Shaun Marler 2021

First Published March 2022

ISBN: 978-0-6450609-0-4

THIS BOOK IS DEDICATED TO THE BELIEVER AND THOSE SEEKING TO UNDERSTAND END-TIME EVENTS AND THE RAPTURE OF THE CHURCH

This book is dedicated to those desiring to grow, in the knowledge and truth of God's Word and the mystery of the 'great catching up' that Paul refers to in his Epistles.

My prayer is that as you carefully read this teaching and study the scripture references given, you will allow the Holy Spirit to birth the revelation of the Word of God on this matter into your spirit.

The Bible says that *"You shall know the truth and the truth shall make you free."* You see, it is a revelation of God's Word birthed in your spirit by the Spirit of God that will bring you victory.

God's will for your life is abundance, love, joy and peace. May this be yours always.

Love in Jesus,
Pastor Shaun

Foreword

I have known Pastor Shaun Marler for over 30 years. I have heard him teach on end-times and The Rapture many times, and each time he has revealed more revelation. He has been internationally recognised by prominent end-time teachers as one having unique revelation on the 'catching away of the church' and the final years of The Tribulation,

I highly recommend his new book on The Rapture. I found many interesting nuggets of gold within its pages!

Revivalist Chris Harvey

We found The Rapture book very simple and easy to digest. It carries incredible valuable scriptural insights into a topic that many steer clear of.

The rapture book by Dr Shaun Marler has critical information for the current days we are living in. This rapture book brings great comfort and is brimming with hope for all believers as we patiently await our Lord's return.

We also believe this book is very prophetic in this hour. God is using Dr Shaun Marler as a powerful prophetic voice in these last end days.

Daniel & Chelsea Hagen
Fire Church Ministries Inc
Australia

Acknowledgements

I would like to acknowledge some of God's great Generals, such as Hilton Sutton, Charles Capps, Lester Sumrall, Marvin Ford, Don Gossett and Drummond Thom. They have now all been promoted to glory and are with their Lord and Saviour Jesus Christ, enjoying the rewards of their faithful service to the Kingdom of God.

These men, whom I have had the pleasure of hosting in our church in Brisbane, Australia, all had a close relationship with Jesus Christ. I was privileged to have met these men, getting to spend time with them, drawing on their anointing and learning from their years of study in the holy scripture. These Generals in the Faith left a legacy of books, writings and bible studies. Through these messages and their personal ministry, they imparted themselves to the next generation of believers. They passed the baton so we could continue to run the race to the finish line. I write this book to you today, the seeker and the believer, encouraging you to lift your eyes and voice in prayer to the soon returning King! Should I myself pass on before His return, then pick up the baton for your generation and finish strong! God bless, *Ps. Shaun.*

Thank You

I would like to give a special thank you to all those who helped in the preparation of this book. Firstly my wife Kerrie, for always believing and encouraging me, her edits and suggestions. Thank you to Jeanie Stone for her proofreading. Thanks also to Sarah Freeman for formatting the book and designing the cover. Plus, Chris Harvey for his cover suggestions, foreword and review.

I would also like to thank the faithful members of my church congregation at World Harvest Ministries. To whom I have had the great joy and privilege of sharing God's word to now for over forty years. You know who you are. Thank you for believing in me, encouraging me, drawing out of me the good word of God and revelations (kisses from the Father) that I have received over the years.

You have inspired me to press in, to keep on studying, learning more and teaching you, your children and others, what I have learned and received from our Lord.

You will always be in my heart.

Purpose of Book

This book is designed to encourage you to prepare for the next greatest event in human history, the Rapture of the Church. Remember the teachings of Jesus and occupy till He comes; busy oneself, trade, study, and be witnesses for the Lord Jesus Christ. Work and minister where He places you in life and stay alert. Plan your life like Jesus is not coming for 100 years, but live life like He's coming tonight. Remember, God needs believers in all walks of life to be a witness for Him. At school, at college, at graduation, at work, and at home; Getting the Word of God into all the world for a witness. Warn others to be ready for this event. No person knows the day or the hour of Jesus' return. He is coming like a thief in the night and one day we will be gone to be with Him.

In Luke 19:12,13, *"He said therefore, A certain nobleman went into a far country to receive for himself a kingdom, and to return. And he called his ten servants, and delivered them ten pounds, and said unto them, Occupy till I come."*

We're instructed in the above verse to occupy till Jesus returns. In the Greek, the word "occupy" gives us the meaning "to trade and be about our Master's business". Our Lord does not want us dropping out of life because of any end-time teaching. He wants us to occupy. He wants us to reign and rule. He wants us to be busy about our Father's business, using all the resources that He has given us to win souls and make disciples. We are to be insulated from the world, not isolated. Each day as we go about our lives, we rub shoulders and touch the lives of people in our schools, workplaces, recreational activities and just living life in general. These people need Jesus. Don't drop out of life, seek the Lord and be a shining example, an ambassador of Christ, living in victory right where you are. Be led by the Spirit, be diligent, believe to excel in all that you do, until the day Jesus comes to gather us all to Himself.

As Jesus said, you watch the skies for signs to determine what the weather will be like. So I encourage you to watch for the signs of His return. The Biblical Prophetic calendar is fast being fulfilled.

As His disciples, let's work together to get the Word of God out into all the world for a witness, preparing for the rapture and then the second coming of Christ.

God Bless,

Pastor Shaun

HELPFUL HINTS TO GAIN
THE MOST FROM THIS BOOK

Study the scriptures carefully.

Read the scriptures in covenant context, chapter context and verse context.

Pray and meditate on the Word in your mind. Think about it.

Be like the Saints in Berea. Acts 17:11 says, *"These were more noble than those in Thessalonica, in that they received the word with all readiness of mind, and searched the scriptures daily, whether those things were so."*

Occupy till He comes. A wise man once said, *"Plan your life like Jesus is not coming for one hundred years but live like He's coming today."*

"Nevertheless when the Son of Man comes, shall he find faith on the earth?" Luke 18:8.

Contents

Introduction 17
Chapter One VISIONS OF RAPTURE 23
Chapter Two PARABLE OF TEN VIRGINS 31
Chapter Three THE LAST GENERATION 39
Chapter Four THINGS TO LOOK FOR 53
Chapter Five THE RAPTURE 69
Chapter Six PEACE AND SAFETY 73
Chapter Seven FAITH - THE VITAL INGREDIENT 79
Chapter Eight THE GREAT ESCAPE 85
Chapter Nine THE CHURCH BEFORE THE THRONE 95
Chapter Ten RAPTURES FIVE, SIX AND SEVEN 101
Chapter Eleven RAPTURE EXPLAINED 117
Chapter Twelve THE FOUR HORSES OF THE APOCALYPSE 131
Chapter Thirteen JUDGEMENT AND MERCY 141
Chapter Fourteen MY DREAM 147
Chapter Fifteen THE RAPTURE, AS REVEALED IN THE ANCIENT JEWISH WEDDING 159
Chapter Sixteen JESUS WILL RETURN 229
Chapter Seventeen TIMELINES 239
Footnotes 276

THE RAPTURE OF THE CHURCH

INTRODUCTION

I believe that if there ever was a day when a book was needed on the Rapture of the Church, it is this day. Because this age, this generation, is going to see and experience the Rapture of the Church, and we don't want to be left behind. Do we?

We don't want to go through the Tribulation, or any part of it. We want to be out of here before it even starts. And one of the greatest promises of God is that He hasn't destined His church to His great end-time judgement that is coming on this world.

> *"Now the Spirit speaks expressly, that in the latter times some shall depart from the faith, giving heed to seducing spirits, and doctrines of devils;"* (1 Timothy 4:1).

There are doctrines going around right now stating that there is not going to be a Rapture.

I am writing a book on this subject, because people need to know the truth concerning God's end-time judgement and the Rapture of His church.

There's teaching being spread now that the Rapture is not happening. There's teaching that we are already in the millennial reign of the Lord Jesus Christ. There is no way possible that we could be in the millennial reign of the Lord Jesus Christ. There is too much pain and suffering in the land.

One only has to turn on the television, or pick up the morning newspaper and read a few lines, or Google 'breaking world news', to know that we are not in the millennial reign, which promises great peace on earth and righteousness reigning in the land, ending all wars.

You only have to look at the worldwide loss of life, destruction of businesses and livelihoods. The huge mental, emotional and financial cost that this Corona pandemic has caused in the nations, and we can know for sure this is not the millennial age that we are currently in. That thousand years of peace is still yet to come.

I believe (and I know some people won't like this, but) if we preach against healing, we don't get healed. If we preach against prosperity, we won't prosper. God is a rewarder, not a destroyer of those that seek Him. Hosea 4:6 tells us that God's people are destroyed by a lack of knowledge. It's not God that is out to destroy His Church, it's Satan. And sometimes, Satan uses our lack of knowledge of God's Word as a weapon against us. The Bible tells us in Proverbs chapter 11 verse 9 that through knowledge shall the just be delivered.

You can only receive a promise of God according to your faith. The Bible says;

> *"But without faith it is impossible to please him: for he that comes to God must believe that he is, and that he is a rewarder of them that diligently seek Him"* (Hebrews 11:6).

> *"My people are destroyed for lack of knowledge: because you have rejected knowledge, I will also reject you, that you shall be no priest to me: seeing you have forgotten the law of thy God, I will also forget your children"* (Hosea 4:6).

'My people perish for lack of knowledge'. The churches that don't preach healing, have people perishing for lack of teaching on healing. The churches that don't teach prosperity, have people perishing for lack of teaching on prosperity.

That is why I believe this teaching on the Rapture is imperative, to impart understanding, knowledge and expectation for this great event.

The Word says, *"By faith we are saved."* The Word also says that, *"Faith comes by hearing and hearing by the Word of God."* This is why I am bringing this teaching to you, to build your faith in God's ability to catch us all up (rapture) to His presence in the pre-ordained time and plan of God.

What about baby Christians? Well, I believe that God is a God of love, and in His grace and wisdom, knows where every person is at in their walk with Him. He is not going to leave behind a person who gets born-again, but hasn't had the opportunity to study all of the doctrines of God. If they are seeking first the Kingdom of God and looking forward to the coming of Jesus, and have a heart towards God and are prayerfully seeking Him, they will go in the Rapture. Remember God is the God of salvation and He loves you. He died so that you could be with Him forever.

I encourage you to repent and get your life right and walk with God in faith now. I firmly believe that if we live 'life ready' for Jesus by seeking first His kingdom and its righteousness, we will be 'Rapture ready'.

I am presenting this book to take away your fear of end times, building faith in your life and spirit through the teachings of Jesus and God's word concerning these times. God promises to never leave us or forsake us. He reveals himself again and again, in His word, as the God who delivers His people from trouble and tribulation. He never changes.

Remember, we receive the blessings of God by faith, and the Bible tells us over and over, 'that He is coming for those that are looking for His coming.'

> *"So Christ was once offered to bear the sins of many; and unto them that look for him shall he appear the second time without sin unto salvation"* (Hebrews 9:28).

N.B. Who went into the ark with Noah? Was it not just his family that believed and walked with God?

> *"Let us therefore fear, lest, a promise being left us of entering into his rest, any of you should seem to come short of it. For unto us was the gospel preached, as well as unto them: but the word preached did not profit them, not being mixed with faith in them that heard it. For we which have believed do enter into rest, as he said, As I have sworn in my wrath, if they shall enter into my rest: although the works were finished from the foundation of the world. For he spoke in a certain place of the seventh day on this wise, And God did rest the seventh day from all his works. And in this place again, If they shall enter into my rest. Seeing therefore it remains that some must enter therein, and they to whom it was first preached entered not in because of unbelief"* (Hebrews 4:1-6).

Once again, we can see that unbelief was the force that prevented some from entering into the promised land. Let's not be guilty of this sin.

> *"Watch ye therefore, and pray always, that ye may be accounted worthy to <u>escape</u> all these things that shall come to pass, and to stand before the Son of man"* (Luke 21:36).

The word escape means *'to flee out of or to be taken away from; to flee away from something.'* The obedient Believers who are watching and praying for His return, will escape the Great Tribulation by going in The Rapture or catching up of the church.

Chapter One

VISIONS OF RAPTURE

My wife is a person whom the Lord will use from time to time, to reveal by revelation or see in a vision, a specific event or set of circumstances. At times when Kerrie has had these visions and shared them with the church or those concerned, people have testified to the accuracy of her visions that pertained to their lives. Others have been set free, while others have received correction or encouragement as well as answers to their needs.

Following, in her own words, is an account of one such supernatural vision she experienced in a Sunday morning church service. While our church was in the midst of worship, God allowed her to see what the rapture would be like.

Kerrie's Vision

One Sunday morning (in 1993), I was standing with the congregation worshipping the Lord. As Shaun started to speak to the people, I sat down in my seat and the next thing I knew, I was floating in space looking down upon the church.

The first thing I thought was, "Why am I here?" I didn't feel at all ill at ease or disturbed in any way. Rather, I just felt totally at peace and secure, and I was over-awed by the beauty of the green planet blowing with the clouds swirling around it and the changes of light on its surface. The whole scene was truly magnificent; the earth, the luminescent moon, the velvety blackness around me, the Milky Way and all the stars. The scene seemed to go on forever, and it was as though all my physical senses were keener and so much more aware and sensitised than what they were on earth. I could actually feel the blackness of the space around me in which I was floating. It's so hard to describe in words, but I actually felt cradled and caressed and overwhelmingly loved and comforted. I felt as though I was actually absorbing all the beauty around me, right into my inner being, as if I was being fed on it. It's very hard to describe this experience. I could have stayed there forever, it was so restful, but as I started to reflect on my purpose for being there, I heard a faint rumbling sound in the distance. Then a small, soft, sweet-smelling breeze brushed against my face and moved my hair back and I closed my eyes and took a deep breath and absorbed it.

I felt enlivened, and took my attention and gaze from the earth below, and looked off into the universe in the direction of the rumbling sound and the breeze. The sound grew louder and louder and the small breeze was now a strong wind which, instead of blowing against me, seemed to be blowing right through me. It didn't make me feel frightened, because in my heart, I knew I had a sense of "knowing" that I was placed there as an observer and I was totally safe.

In a little while, I could see off in the distance what looked, at first sight, to be a huge star rapidly growing in size. In my heart, I knew it wasn't a star, but I didn't know at that point what it was. I continued to watch intently, and the noise grew louder and the wind fiercer. It was as though the whole universe started to move around me, and lights flew by me and were absorbed into this approaching mass. I could see it fully now, a dazzling white/gold, moving, bubbling mass. Extremely bright, and the thought came to me, that if I were in my earthly body, I would have been blinded by it, but I still felt so very much at peace. It was such a shocking sight! I say shocking because I felt as though I'd taken in a huge breath but couldn't let it out again. I was so stunned and amazed and over-awed by it. The mass was gold yet clear and bubbling and growing and absorbing lights into it. Very hard to put into words. It shot past me, and I was aware that the noise and the wind (if it were on earth) would be far greater, stronger, more powerful than any of our worst cyclones or tornadoes. Yet, it blew right through me and though I could feel the intensity of it – I was not at all buffeted by it or frightened or harmed.

As I watched, it shot down and hit the outer atmosphere of the earth. There was a sound like a terrific crack and I could see something like an explosion of light in an instant cover the whole atmosphere of the earth. It looked like white lightning. I knew in my heart that at that moment, there was much fear on earth and surprise in the hearts of people. No one but believers knew what it was.

The whole scene actually happened in a blinking of the eyes, in a brief moment of time, and I was aware that the bubbling mass of light was slowed down deliberately for me to observe it, otherwise, I knew that I would not have seen a thing, so fast was it moving and so fast did it hit the earth's atmosphere and immediately deflect back off into space in the direction that it came.

It was almost like watching a fast-moving film that was slowed down frame by frame to see detail.

I knew when the mass hit the earth that I was witnessing the rapture of God's people, the catching up and taking away of the believing ones. As the scene slowed (so that I could see it), I saw that when the bubbling gold light (which I knew was the Son of God, in spirit form and also angelic beings) hit the earth, it thundered and the noise reverberated around the whole earth, and the rushing wind could be felt everywhere at once. Buildings shook and moved and swayed and some people fainted for fear. Others thought they heard voices. Some were asleep and were awakened by what they thought was an earthquake, others thought it was a cyclone. There was much terror, but no physical damage to the earth except that afterwards, I saw that it no longer rotated smoothly on its axis, but it wobbled like a warped ball rolling unevenly, badly affecting weather patterns, and the moon was much further away than it had been before.

Also, at the same time, I saw the believers, some in bed, some at work, some driving, some walking – all of them going about the ordinary affairs of life. As the time frame slowed still further, I saw that for the first couple of feet off the ground, their bodies rose and they looked just like normal, then it was as though their bodies grew darker and blacker and split from top to toe (this is very, very difficult to describe!) and as I watched I saw that this black outer shell was encompassing the same white, gold, luminescent, bubbling mass that I saw hit the earth's outer atmosphere and deflect back off into outer space. The mass inside (the people) multiplied and enveloped the black outer shell, which all the while was growing thinner and receding. As I watched, I noticed that some were much quicker than others to have the bubbling mass inside them set free and in my heart, I wondered at the black shell outer-casing, which formerly, clearly, was their earthly bodies. It was as though no sooner did I question in my mind, that the question was immediately answered, "This is the heaviness of the mortality". I realised that the bubbling mass of light that I was observing coming out of the believer and enveloping and consuming their mortal casing was their spirit – made out of exactly the same substance as the Son.

Some people (believers) I could see, had only a small and weak amount of this white bubbling light inside them and it glowed, but there was not enough of it to break through the dark casing of their bodies. It was (the casing) so very hard and so very black and I realised at once although these Christians left the ground slightly, they soon fell back, because they were not filled with the power and Spirit of God, that their own spirits were not irradiating the power, that they had lived very selfish lives and their flesh was entrapping their spirits (which in themselves) longed to go up. This was very hard to watch and grievous, for I 'knew' that some believers were being left behind not by divine, sovereign appointment of the Father or Son, but almost as it were that they did not fulfil a natural law and their state of existence on the earth (prior to the rapture) which was of their own choosing, prevented this natural law from acting on their behalf, for their benefit.

The light and power of the Son acted just like a huge magnet which literally sucked up the Spirit of the believers dissolving and encompassing their mortal flesh and totally absorbing them, unifying them into the huge, powerful white, bubbling yet transparent mass of light. I could no longer see individuals but just a larger mass of one-ness.

By way of explanation, if you could visualise a huge magnet coming down and landing on a very thick glass tabletop and other small magnetised objects on the floor underneath the table, suddenly flying up underneath the glass not adhering to the glass, because the glass was shattered and open (like I saw the earth's atmosphere) but coming right through it and adhering to the magnet and other pieces of slightly magnetised material which had felt the pull of the big magnet were standing up on end but were not sufficiently magnetised to be pulled up off the floor, this best describes in natural terms what I saw.

As I said, all these events happened in the twinkling of an eye. If I had blinked and had the whole scene not been slowed down for me to witness, I would not have seen anything, save for hearing the immense crack or clap of thunder reverberating around the whole world. All the inhabitants of the earth heard the sound and were immensely fearful, especially when communications began from nation to nation, back and forth, media and ordinary people contacting loved ones to see if they'd heard what they heard or to ring others just to describe the sound, unaware that the ones they were calling had experienced it also. When it became apparent that it was a simultaneous worldwide event, there was much panic and as if a supernatural fear gripped their hearts. Also, the whole planet, even in broad daylight hours, seemed to be much darker and yet there was no visible obstruction between the sun and the earth. Scientists were keenly looking out into space. Some were saying they saw a bright, huge light swiftly disappearing, and some high-tech equipment gave distorted and differing information. Confusion reigned, and everywhere people were putting forth their ideas on what had happened. Some were saying, a huge meteor brushed by our outer atmosphere and disturbed the electrical fields of the air, others were saying it was a freak of nature, others a cosmic storm brought about by all sorts of weird and wonderful cosmic theories. More and more media, however, were saying that it was the earth's destiny, that it was a good event for the earth, and not a bad one, and that it couldn't be ruled out that some alien force (benevolent) had visited the earth and had taken specimens (people) that were out of harmony, off the planet so that the earth would survive.

It was pointed out that now these people were gone, it was very likely that at last, world peace could now be achieved, and the New World Order would prosper. The people that had left the earth were blamed for everything, from famines to wars and failing economies.

I noticed from out in space, how cold and darker the earth seemed. It no longer looked so beautiful and luminescent, but there was still some light there, but not as before. I could feel the fear and uncertainty coming from off the earth. The next thing I remember was hearing Shaun wind up the end of his sermon, sitting there in my chair. I felt so stunned and yet so excited about what I'd witnessed. I never heard a word of Shaun's sermon though!

Chapter Two

PARABLE OF TEN VIRGINS

Today I believe that if the Church isn't looking for His coming, the Church is going to miss out on His coming.

"Then shall the kingdom of heaven be likened unto ten virgins, which took their lamps, and went forth to meet the bridegroom" (Matthew 25:1).

Then shall the kingdom of heaven be likened unto this. Just like ten virgins who took their lamps, and went forth to meet the bridegroom.

"And five of them were wise, and five were foolish" (Matthew 25:2). They were all saved, part of that kingdom and all born-again. They were all supposed to have been ready but only half were.

"They that were foolish took their lamps, and took no oil with them:" (Matthew 25:3). Now oil always speaks of anointing oil – the Holy Spirit.

> *"But the wise took oil in their vessels with their lamps"* (Matthew 25:4).

So they took extra oil in containers with them.

> *"While the bridegroom tarried, they all slumbered and slept"* (Matthew 25:5).

> *"And at midnight there was a cry made, Behold, the bridegroom comes; go ye out to meet him"* (Matthew 25:6).

If you listen to what the Spirit of God is saying; if you listen to what God is saying, He is saying: *"Behold the bridegroom comes."*

There are people saying that He is not coming. But there are many teachers and preachers of the Word saying and warning, "get your life in order!" He's coming! He's coming! He's coming!

> *"And at midnight there was a cry made, Behold, the bridegroom comes;"* (Matthew 25:6).

If you're listening, that cry is going forth now! I believe we are in the midnight hour.

God reveals His secrets to those that are listening and are tuned in. I believe that if we are praying and seeking God, we know it in our own spirit, that Jesus is coming.

"And at midnight there was a cry made, Behold, the bridegroom cometh; go ye out to meet him" (Matthew 25:6).

They all expected to go.

"Then all those virgins arose, and trimmed their lamps. And the foolish said unto the wise, "Give us of your oil; for our lamps are gone out" (Matthew 25:7-8).

Or in the correct Greek breakdown, it is, our lamps are "going out". It is not that their lamps were never alight, they were alight. They were burning. Yet their lamps weren't burning brightly, they were only just alight and going out due to a lack of oil.

I don't believe that Jesus Christ is going to leave behind a just born-again Christian, who hasn't had time to study all the doctrines of God. It is a heart thing. Is your heart into God's will and word? Do you love the Holy Spirit? Are you fellowshipping with Him? Are you seeking first the Kingdom of God and his righteousness, or is your light fading and going out?

But I do believe that the mature Christian – who has had the time, has had the opportunity to study, to show himself approved unto God, (the Bible says workmen that need not to be ashamed, people who know to rightly divide the Word of God) will have to give an account of what we've done with our time. We're going to have to give an account before Jesus, of where we are in God. We are going to have to give an account for how we are living our lives.

That's the reason why I believe communion is so important. It is a time to refocus, repent and realign our lives to God's plan for us revealed in His Word. It's time to focus on Jesus by watching, praying and being led by the Holy Spirit.

I believe that people who have actively preached against The Rapture, or carried on rebelling in areas of known sin, are going to wake up one day – and the Church is going to be gone. They will be left behind to go through the Tribulation, except they repent and refill their lamps (lives) with the Word and the Holy Spirit, doing the will of God.

These aren't the days to backslide. These aren't the days to be rebellious. These aren't the days to continue in sin. The hour is too late – it's almost midnight. Repent before it is too late and return to your first love for Jesus. Deal with the known areas of sin in your life and put them under the blood of Jesus. Turn from those ways that aren't pleasing to God and walk in paths of righteousness. Ask for God by the power of His Holy Spirit to help you. Remember, you were born again to win and be redeemed in Jesus Christ.

The Christians that are walking by faith and doing all they know to do, to the best of their ability and are walking with the Lord will be raptured and miss out on the whole of this tribulation. We will be gone, caught up with the Lord to be with Him forever.

"And the foolish said unto the wise, give us of your oil; for our lamps are gone out" (Matthew 25:8).

"But the wise answered, saying, Not so; lest there be not enough for us and you: but go ye rather to them that sell, and buy for yourselves." (Matthew 25:9).

In other words, 'you'd just better go and learn these things.' You had better get your life right with God. You had better repent and get your priorities straight. But what happened?

"And while they went to buy, the bridegroom came; and they that were ready went in with him to the marriage: and the door was shut" (Matthew 25:10).

"Afterward came also the other virgins, saying, Lord, Lord, open to us." (Matthew 25:11).

See, they're all saved, they're all born-again of the Spirit of God, they've all had Holy Ghost oil; but their lamps are going out because they've started to depart from the faith. Giving heed to seducing spirits, and doctrines of devils, and teaching like there is going to be no Rapture, or that we're in the millennium now, or other such ridiculous stuff, or just simply backsliding and turning away from the things of the Lord and His Word. Living their lives serving their own selfish desires instead of serving the Lord and His church.

"Afterward came also the other virgins, saying Lord, Lord, open to us. But he answered and said, Verily I say unto you, I know you not. Watch therefore, for ye

know neither the day nor the hour wherein the Son of man cometh" (Matthew 25:11-13).

Watch Therefore

"For the kingdom of heaven is as a man travelling into a far country, who called his own servants, and delivered unto them his goods" (Matthew 25:14).

"And unto one he gave five talents, to another two, and to another one; to every man according to his several ability; and straightway took his journey" (Matthew 25:15).

The person that had five talents, went and used them and profited for the kingdom of God. But one of them buried his talents, and this is what some of the Church is doing now. A portion of the church is becoming complacent. Many are in disobedience to God, not serving Him and others are forsaking the assembling of the body of Christ or church gatherings. They are not in fellowship with other Christians. We are warned about this in the book of Hebrews 10:25.

"Not forsaking the assembling of ourselves together, as the manner of some is; but exhorting one another: and so much the more, as ye see the day approaching" (Hebrews 10:25).

Where possible, we must meet together and encourage each other. Pray for each other. Help and uphold each other to stay in the faith and will of God, while we wait, looking for His return. It is in the assembling that we can serve and love each other.

Some members are falling into sin and refusing to repent in spite of all the prompting and convictions of their hearts. God doesn't want any of His children to go through the Tribulation. The Tribulation is God's time of great judgement poured out on the earth because of all the wickedness of mankind. When the church is gone, evil will run rampant, because God would have removed the restraining force. This force that restrains the evil one and the Anti-Christ spirit, is the prayers of the saints through the Word, by the power of the Holy Spirit and the mighty name of Jesus. The church has the power to bind and loose and to take authority over the works of Satan. When the church is raptured, nature itself will be totally out of control and the stars of heaven will be falling upon the earth. You don't want to be here for that time of Tribulation judgement.

Chapter Three

THE LAST GENERATION

"And when these things begin to come to pass, then look up, and lift up your heads: for your redemption draweth nigh" (Luke 21:28).

What things? The things that Jesus has just outlined. We'll go back to verse 24 in this chapter.

"And they shall fall by the edge of the sword, and shall be led away captive into all nations: and Jerusalem shall be trodden down of the Gentiles, until the times of the Gentiles be fulfilled" (Luke 21:24).

The time of the Gentiles is totally fulfilled at the Rapture of the Church.

Two thousand years ago, the nation of Israel rejected Jesus Christ as their Lord and Saviour. The book of Hosea in Chapter 4:6 reveals, *"...because thou hast rejected knowledge, I will also reject thee, that thou shalt be no priest to me:..."*, the nation of Israel, as a whole, rejected Jesus Christ as their Lord and Saviour. The people called for Jesus, their Messiah, to be crucified and they asked for Barabbas to be set free.

> *"But the chief priests and elders persuaded the multitude that they should ask Barabbas, and destroy Jesus. The governor answered and said unto them, Which of the two would you have me release for you? They said, Barabbas. Pilate said unto them, What shall I do then with Jesus who is called Christ? They all say to him, Let him be crucified. And the governor said, Why, what evil has he done? But they cried out the more, saying, Let him be crucified"* (Matthew 27:20-23).

Jesus was crucified and died on the cross for His people and for the sins of the whole world, that is you and I.

For the next 2000 years, the Jews would be led away, captive into all nations of the earth, exiled from their own homeland until 1948.

> *"Who hath heard such a thing? who hath seen such things? Shall the earth be made to bring forth in one day? or shall a nation be born at once? for as soon as Zion travailed, she brought forth her children"* (Isaiah 66:8).

It was on the day of May 14th in 1948, 70+ years ago, that Israel became a nation again. The Bible says *"And they shall fall by the edge of the sword,..."* and this has been the last 2000 years of Jewish history.

Luke 21:24 says, *"...and Jerusalem shall be trodden down of the Gentiles, until the times of the Gentiles be fulfilled."*

In June 1967, Israel was once again compelled to fight for its existence. Israel succeeded against all odds and prevailed over the armies of it's three most powerful neighbours, which threatened to strangle it from the south, east and north.

The following day, 7th June 1967 (28 Iyar 5727), Israel captured the Old City of Jerusalem.

So here we can see, when Jerusalem came back under Israel's control, the scripture above in the book of Luke was fulfilled. This marked the times of the Gentiles (church age) being fulfilled.

Hosea 4:6 says, *'because you've rejected me, I'll reject you.'* Hosea 6:2 declares *'After two days will he revive us: in the third day he will raise us up, and we shall live in his sight."*

The two days referred to here, is the time period of two thousand years, or what is now known as the Church Age, the Age of Grace. The third day is a reference to the one thousand years millennial reign of Christ. This will be the day of Christ, which starts at the second coming of Jesus Christ and lasts for one thousand years or one day.

The second coming starts at the end of the time of the Tribulation. This is also known as Daniel's Seventieth Week, Jacob's Trouble and is a period of seven years. This tribulation begins after the Rapture of the church, which happens at the end of the two days or two thousand year time period.

From 2 Peter 3:8, we can see that a day is a thousand years, and a thousand years is a day.

"But, beloved, be not ignorant of this one thing, that one day is with the Lord as a thousand years, and a thousand years as one day" (2 Peter 3:8).

So what we are prophetically seeing here is, the last two thousand years of Israel's history. We see scripture being fulfilled. Israel being led away captive, Jerusalem being trodden down of the Gentiles. The Jewish nation falling by the edge of the sword until the time of the Gentiles be fulfilled, as the new nation of Israel retakes the old city.

At the Holocaust, the genocide of European Jews during World War II, by Hilter and Nazi Germany. Between 1941 and 1945, around six million Jewish people were killed.

Then in 1948, a miracle of miracles happened, and Israel became a nation again. In 1967 they retook the old city. Remember what God had promised in His Word? After two days, or two thousand years, I will revive the Jewish nation. As stated above, Jerusalem was taken back in 1967. Then in 2017, on 6th December, the United States recognized Jerusalem as the capital of Israel, under the leadership of President Donald Trump.

"And when these things begin to come to pass, then look up, and lift up your heads; for your redemption draws nigh" (Luke 21:28).

What things begin to come to pass? When Jerusalem is no longer trodden down of the Gentiles. But what we have, in God's timetable of things, is an overlapping of time. Things prophetically are coming to pass now at a rapid pace. We are at the end of the Church Age, in the final days before the Rapture of the church. After the Rapture of the church, God will restart the Jewish prophetic time clock and Daniel's Seventieth Week, the last week of his end-time prophecy, which concludes with the second coming of Jesus and the battle of Armageddon.

Daniel's Seventieth Week, is a time period of seven years, also known as the Tribulation. The second three and half years of the Tribulation is far worse than the first three and half years. The second three and half years, is known as the Great Tribulation. After this time, Jesus will return and the one thousand-year reign of Christ on this planet will begin.

We are currently at the time of this writing in the closing days/years of the church age. The church was born on the day of Pentecost, approximately two thousand years ago. God has promised two thousand years or two days for the church age.

From 2 Peter 3:8, we can see that a thousand years as one day to God and one day a thousand. God is reviving the Jewish nation and the beginning of this marked the start of the last generation for all things to be fulfilled. Then would come the second advent or return of Christ and His millennial reign, which will be one day or a thousand years long.

God has revived the nation of Israel and as the church age draws to a close, we will see the last of Daniel's seventieth week played out.

I like to describe it this way, sixty-nine weeks of Daniel's seventy weeks concluded with the death and resurrection of our Lord Jesus Christ. At that point in time, God stopped the Jewish time clock and He slotted in the church age. The Age of Grace was to last two thousand years. This time would culminate with the Rapture of the Church or the catching away of the church. This is described in the book of 1 Thessalonians 4:16-17.

> *"For the Lord himself shall descend from heaven with a shout, with the voice of the archangel, and with the trump of God: and the dead in Christ shall rise first: Then we which are alive and remain shall be caught up together with them in the clouds, to meet the Lord in the air: and so shall we ever be with the Lord."*

The Jewish time clock, as I refer to it, or the last of Daniel's seventieth week, will start to tick off sometime after the Rapture, the close of the church age at the Rapture of the church. No one knows the day or the hour that this Rapture will take place, but we have the major sign of the time given to us by the Lord Jesus Christ himself.

In Luke 21:29 it says, *"And he spake to them a parable; Behold the fig tree,..."* (this is a reference to the nation of Israel) *"...and all the trees;"* (all other nations).

> "When they now shoot forth, ye see and know of your own selves that summer is now nigh at hand. So likewise ye, when ye see these things come to pass, know ye that the kingdom of God is nigh at hand" (Luke 21:30-31).

The Kingdom of God, as mentioned here, is a reference to the millennial reign of the Lord Jesus Christ, also known as the Day of Christ. As stated previously in this chapter, it will be one thousand years long. After this will come the Great White Throne judgement of God spoken about in Revelation chapter 20. Then God will create a new heaven and new earth.

In Hosea 6:2, it says that after two days He would revive them; in the third day, He would raise them up to live in His sight. That's the millennial reign. That's not upon us yet, but it's nearly upon us. That hasn't started yet, but it's going to start very soon.

> "After two days will he revive us: in the third day he will raise us up, and we shall live in his sight" (Hosea 6:2).

At the second coming or second advent of the Lord Jesus Christ, after the Rapture of the Church and the seven years of Tribulation, known as Daniel's seventieth week, Jesus will set-up His Kingdom on earth and reign for a thousand years from Jerusalem.

> "...for out of Zion shall go forth the law, and the word of the Lord from Jerusalem:" (Isaiah 2:3).

"And he spake to them a parable; Behold the fig tree, and all the trees; When they now shoot forth, ye see and know of your own selves that summer is now nigh at hand. So likewise ye, when ye see these things come to pass, know ye that the kingdom of God is nigh at hand" (Luke 21:29-31).

What things? *'And Jerusalem shall be trodden down of the Gentiles, until the time of the Gentiles be fulfilled"* (Luke 21:24b).

I believe that when Jesus was referring to the fig tree, as stated, He was referring to the rebirth of Israel. He went on to say, "The fig tree and all the trees." I believe that Jesus was referring to all the nations gaining their sovereignty and independence. In the last 100 years, we have seen the birth or the rebirth of so many nations.

After World War 1, the Ottoman Empire was dismantled by treaty and came to an end in 1922. From that time, we have seen the Colonial Empire's breakup and the dismantling of the Soviet Union. Now many nations have become nations in their own right.

In 1943 Lebanon or the cedar tree was re-established as a country. Also that year, Syria, the olive tree, along with Jordan the palm tree in 1946, and just prior to this, the kingdom of Saudi Arabia, the date palm in 1932. As we know, Israel, the fig tree, was reborn on the 14th May 1948. Since then, we have seen nation after nation become self-ruling and gaining their independence.

On the 25th of December 1991, the Soviet hammer and sickle flag lowered for the last time over the Kremlin, thereafter replaced by the Russian tri-colour. Earlier in the day, Mikhail Gorbachev resigned his post as president of the Soviet Union, leaving Boris Yeltsin as president of the newly independent Russian state. The then-current American President Bush recognized all twelve independent republics and established diplomatic relations with Russia, Ukraine, Belarus, Kazakhstan, Armenia and Kyrgyzstan. Then in February 1992, American diplomats visited the remaining republics, and diplomatic relations were established with Uzbekistan, Moldova, Azerbaijan, Turkmenistan, and Tajikistan. At the time, a civil war was happening in Georgia preventing its recognition.

The French Colonial Empire, one of the largest empires in history, broke up, and even the small island nation of Vanuatu gained it's independence in 1980. There is little left of the British Empire, which at it's height was the largest in history.

The Suez crisis confirmed Britain's decline as a global power and the transfer of Hong Kong to China in 1997. This marked for many, the end of the British Empire. Although fourteen overseas territories still remain under British sovereignty.

The point that I wanted us to see here was when Jesus spoke of the fig tree becoming a nation again, and then His reference to all the other trees, is that nations are often referred to or have a tree as their identity. Syrian olive trees, Saudi Arabian date trees etc. Our generation has seen the breakup of these empires, and more nations have gained their sovereignty and independence than at any other time in history.

"*Verily I say unto you, This generation...*" (Luke 21:32). What generation? The generation that sees Jerusalem no longer being trodden down of the Gentiles, and restored as the capital of Israel. The generation that sees the resurrection of the nation of Israel. "*Verily I say unto you, This generation shall not pass away, till all be fulfilled*" (Luke 21:32).

Scholars tell us the Jewish generation is somewhere between seventy and eighty years long. It could be even up to a hundred years long. I like to think of a generation as a family made up of babies to great-grandparents. This then would be around one hundred years. So we have a generation that Jesus spoke of, as a period of time from seventy to a hundred years. Jesus said the generation that sees all of these things coming to pass would be the last generation before His second coming and the great redemption of believers to heaven at the Rapture.

Mans Days as Allotted by God

> "*The days of our years are threescore years and ten; and if by reason of strength they be fourscore years, yet is their strength labour and sorrow; for it is soon cut off, and we fly away. Who knows the power of thine anger? even according to your fear, so is your wrath. So teach us to number our days, that we may apply our hearts unto wisdom. Return, O Lord, how long? and let it repent thee concerning your servants*" (Psalm 90:10-13).

Here in this Psalm of Moses, we can see a beautiful picture of the last generation, the Rapture of the Church, the time of Jacob's trouble (Daniel's seventieth week) when God pours out His wrath. We then see how God shortens the time for His servant's sake (this will be the remnant of Israel and those saved during the Tribulation, followed by His return to establish His millennial reign, declaring His works to all).

Still today, the average worldwide life span is 72.6 years for mankind. Some countries are slightly higher and others lower. I believe we as believers under the blessing of Abraham can live longer lifespans because God promised to satisfy His children with long life. I just wanted to show you how the time span for mankind given by God at the time of Moses' writing is still completely relevant today.

So you can see, from God's prophetic timetable, we are the last generation that Jesus spoke about. All of these things began to come to pass at the end of the two day period of time, when Israel was re-birthed. We are in the closing days of the two thousand year Church Age. We are living in the times and fulfilment of the revival of the Jewish nation and the land of Israel.

People ask me, what will we be doing for seven years in heaven after the Rapture? I believe we're going to be taught how to reign and how to rule. We're being taught now, but there, we'll be getting first-hand teaching from the Lord Jesus Christ Himself, getting ready to return with Him as part of His armies from heaven at His second coming.

We are seeing the prophetic end time events as foretold in the Word unfold before our eyes. We are seeing the beginnings of the Anti-Christ kingdom agenda rising to power. When the Anti-Christ rises to power, he will confirm a covenant, peace treaty with Israel for seven years. This will be after the Rapture of the Church to heaven. The Anti-Christ will break that covenant in the middle of that seven-year period of time. He will absolutely ransack the nation of Israel for 3½ years or forty-two months (½ of a week as Daniel records in his writings in chapter nine of the book of Daniel, confirmed in Revelation 13:5). His rule will cease at the Battle of Armageddon when Jesus returns at His second coming. Jesus defeats the Anti-Christ and the false prophet and casts them into the lake of fire. The Lord Jesus Christ will then set up His thousand-year reign of prosperity and peace.

N.B. A careful study of the book of Daniel and historical time frames renders Daniel's prophecies as 1 week = 7 years.

When Jesus returns at His second coming, the battle of Armageddon will take place. The greatest army that the world has ever been amassed on the face of the earth, to try and stop the returning King of Kings and Lord of Lords. Jesus will annihilate this army with the brightness of His presence and the sword of His mouth, which is the Word of God!

The Lord Jesus will take possession of this earth and reign as King of Kings and Lord of Lords in righteousness. We then shall reign and be with Him for one thousand years. And I believe this is about to come to pass, very, very soon.

When Jesus says in Luke 21:28, *"look up, and lift up your heads; for your redemption draweth nigh"*, He is actually saying 'lift up yourselves because of a reason of elated, joyous expectation and preparation of an event.' The Greek word means to 'lift one's self up by reason of elated joy! And that is what we are doing, 'lifting ourselves up by reason of elated, joyous expectation and preparation of an event', the Rapture of the Church.

That's why we preach the Rapture, so we can prepare the Church, so we can prepare ourselves, so we can teach how close it is, so that others can be prepared for this hour.

Some might say, 'well, I don't believe it's going to happen in my generation.' 'I don't believe this is the last generation.' Well, whichever way you look at it, this is your last generation.

I believe with all of my heart. I'm persuaded. I'm convinced. This is the last generation! I'm convinced that these are the remaining years, the last few years, of the last generation.

So what are we to do? We are to lift up ourselves by reason of elated, joyous expectation. I don't care what the TV says. I don't care what the news media says. I don't care what this world says. I'm lifting up myself with great expectation, and with great joy, because I am preparing myself for the return of the Lord Jesus Christ and the Rapture of the Church.

Be prepared! We must be prepared, we must be watching. It doesn't mean we walk around looking up in the sky for Jesus. It means to watch the signs of the times. When you see these things come to pass. Now, we have seen the formation of the E.C.. At the signing of the Treaty of Rome, in 1957, the foundation of the E.C. was laid. That's when it was conceived, and the Book of Revelation tells us that the Roman Empire shall be resurrected. Revelation 13:3, we are seeing that come together: in the same geographical area occupied by the old Roman Empire.

The world is gearing up in preparation for the Anti-Christ who will reign over the ten kings from the old Roman Empire Region.

When you see these "things!" – When you see Israel become a nation; you see them take the old city; you see the signs of the times. These are the things that we are watching for. These are the things that are showing us that the return of the Lord Jesus Christ is very close at hand.

What else do we look for as a major sign of His return?

"REVIVAL" and the Gospel being preached to all nations for a witness and warning.

Friends, I believe with all of my heart that Jesus is coming soon, but even if I am wrong and His coming is delayed. If you live Rapture Ready, praying, seeking first His Kingdom and His righteousness, you will also live life ready. Let us all repent and return to our first love. Let us all be ready to give an account to any other person what is the hope that is within us, sharing the gospel of salvation and the message of God's love with any and all who would listen. Let us occupy until He comes doing trade and business, planning our lives like He is not coming for a hundred years but living our lives like He is coming tonight.

Chapter Four

Things to Look For

There are three things that we look for. It says in Matthew 24:6,7,8.

> *"And you shall hear of wars and rumours of wars: see that you be not troubled: for all these things must come to pass, but the end is not yet. For nation shall rise against nation, and kingdom against kingdom: and there shall be famines, and pestilences, and earthquakes, in divers places. All these are the beginning of sorrows."*

Jesus told us very plainly that in the last days, there's going to be: wars, rumours of wars; terrible earthquakes, famines, in diverse places around the Earth; the beginning of sorrows. All of these things are going to escalate. We are seeing this each time there is a volcano, an earthquake, or a hurricane. It seems to be the biggest and the worst there's been. There is an escalation in natural disasters. The world weather pattern has changed, and is growing worse than before. This is what Jesus said, we can expect these things.

The Holy Spirit says this is what will happen in the last days, *'some will depart from the faith, giving heed to doctrines of devils and seducing spirits.'* We're seeing people depart from the faith. People are becoming lovers of self more than lovers of God. We have even created the new word "selfie". Social media is becoming an obsession for many people. People are becoming lovers of self more than lovers of God. Of course, God wants us to look after our bodies, but not at the expense of our relationship with Him, our fellow Christians or our family.

All believers are looking forward to the millennium. The Bible describes the millennium as a time of great global prosperity. A time when there's no death. Our Bibles teach us that the whole earth is filled with the knowledge of the Glory of God. During this time, a child isn't considered an adult until he is 100 years old, because we will all live for 1000 years, and the Christians will reign and rule with Jesus. Think about that, people are not mature until you're 100 years old in the millennium. The Christians will be like Jesus during this time with their resurrected, eternal bodies.

What are the End Times signs? Let's read what the Spirit says concerning the end times. What does the Spirit of God say concerning the End Times signs?

> *"The Spirit of God speaks expressly that in the latter days, some will depart from the faith, giving heed to seducing spirits and doctrines of devils"* (1 Timothy 4:1).

That then is a warning from the Holy Spirit. That there is going to come false doctrines in the last days and seducing spirits to deceive people. Jesus also referred to this great last day deception in His teachings. He stated that even the elect would be deceived, if that were possible. This shows the extent and effectiveness of these spirits on peoples' minds in the last days.

The escalation of occult teachings, occult practices: you can see on the current affairs TV programs, how in Europe and other places, the heads of some companies are enquiring of astrologers and mediums before making their business decisions. Even some big multi-national companies are employing astrologers, fortune tellers to enquire for them, before making their business plans. On the northern coast of Brisbane, where I live, there is now a Satanic temple, where they practice the worship of Satan. They are even trying to get Satanism, taught in a school as a religion.

The Bible says the Spirit speaks expressly. There is going to come this deception, to where even some Christians would depart from the faith-- giving heed to seducing spirits and doctrines of devils. Just look at the news media over a period of time, read the newspapers, watch the television, and you will even see, sad to say, preachers coming out and denying that the Bible is the infallible Word of God. Saying such things as, the virgin birth is a fable, etc.

The Word of God is coming under great attack from seducing spirits and doctrines of devils; some Believers have departed from the faith, and no longer follow Jesus. This in itself is another end-time sign. We are seeing a rise in the occult, cults and the New Age Movement.

Under the Old Covenant, the old Kings, or captains, if they departed from the faith, would enquire of mediums. Nebuchadnezzar, the King of Babylon, had his sorcerers, his wizards, and his magicians; they were always enquiring into the supernatural realm. That is happening right now, in our day and age, when multi-national companies are employing these people to advise them on their business decisions. We don't need that. God can give us the wisdom, through the Gifts of the Spirit. Those things are a counterfeit of the true gifts of the Spirit. The Bible says, if we will hearken unto the Lord our God, He would teach us to profit. God wants us to do well, He wants to bless us, making our lives and businesses profitable. God desires us to do well. He wants us to make the right business decisions. He wants you to prosper.

> *"Beloved, I wish above all things that you may prosper and be in health, even as your soul prospers"* (3 John 2).

Jesus says, concerning the signs of the last days, that there would be an escalation in natural upheavals. We're definitely seeing this. I can't remember a time like the present, where it seems every week there is a major catastrophe in the natural realm on the earth. A hurricane, a cyclone, a flood, an earthquake, wildfires, a pestilence, a plague, or some great drought causing a food shortage or famine. Now the whole world is facing the Corona pandemic and its consequences. The Apostle Paul said, *"In the last days there would be perilous times"* (2 Timothy 3:1).

The word 'perilous' in the scripture above, comes from a Greek word meaning "injurious times, hard to cope with, difficult times, dangerous times." I believe that we can all agree that this describes what the nations are facing today. The coronavirus has affected every nation on earth. We as believers must pray for our leaders to have God's wisdom to deal with these times.

We must pray against Satan using these circumstances to steal our God-given freedoms and way of life. Jesus came to set the captives free. He taught us, as believers, that we are to pray for everyone in authority and for all people to be saved and come to the knowledge of the truth. When we are aware that there will be seducing spirits released in the last days and one of their strategies is to cause great deception in the land, we can pray more effectively. We need our leaders (of the nations) to deal with these national calamities, in a way that is not against the principles of God, as laid out in the Word or injurious to our way of life. Hence as Believers, Jesus stressed that we must watch in prayer. The prayers of the Saints are powerful to keep the blessing of God on a nation and it's people, until the Rapture of the Church.

Jesus says that these things would be known as the beginning of sorrows, when we see them increase, it would be a sign that we are entering into the end days of this current Dispensation of Grace (church age), when natural disasters increase, when these calamities increase greatly on our planet, in the end times. They would be like neon lights or LED boards, warning us of the approaching Great Tribulation and pending judgement of God. It would be a sign that the times are wrapping up. Not the end of the world. The Bible shows us this world has got another 1000 years to go yet. Another 1000 years, before God creates a new heaven and a new earth. Where He brings

His people into the new heaven and the new earth, but that will be after the millennial reign of the Lord Jesus Christ. The time when Jesus will return and run this planet for 1000 years. That's good to look forward to, isn't it?

Do you know why it is so good to look forward to? Because if you're born of the Spirit of the Living God, you get to reign and rule with Him.

You see Judges on the television, and you hear these Court decisions passed down, and sometimes you see the injustice of this "World's system"; the Bible says the cries of the innocent have come unto the Father. God is long-suffering. He's not slack concerning His promise to send back the Lord Jesus Christ, to bring in righteousness and right judgement. He is long-suffering because He is not willing that any should perish. He is not a slack God. The cries of the innocent have come unto the Father, and He is soon going to move by the might of His hand. He is going to take His Church out of this planet, and then pour out His righteous judgement.

Prepare Yourself for Revival

Revival is a new beginning of obedience to God.

We will have Revival before the Great Tribulation takes place. The awakened church is filling their lamps with the Word and Spirit and they are crying for revival. As far as the world is concerned, the prophecies have been fulfilled, allowing Jesus Christ to come at any minute. The world's in the biggest mess it has ever been in since creation. However, I believe prophecy so far as the Church is concerned, isn't totally fulfilled yet. We are still going to have a mighty Revival. God says, in the book of Haggai that, "He is going to shake all nations and the desire of all nations will come." What God desires from the nations is the souls of men and women that Jesus died for. In our Father's house are many mansions and Jesus is preparing a place for us.

> *"For thus says the Lord of hosts; Yet once, it is a little while, and I will shake the heavens, and the earth, and the sea, and the dry land; And I will shake all nations, and the desire of all nations shall come: and I will fill this house with glory, saith the Lord of hosts. The silver is mine, and the gold is mine, saith the Lord of hosts. The glory of this latter house shall be greater than of the former, says the Lord of hosts: and in this place will I give peace, saith the Lord of hosts"* (Haggai 2:6-9).

I believe that we are in the time of shaking as spoken of here in the book of Haggai. If the Church is going to see this great revival, an increased glory on the people of God. Then the Church is going to have to get their lamps filled by repenting and turning to their first love, for God and His kingdom. We are going to have to pray, seeking His face and getting busy about our Father's business, winning souls.

The spirit says that false teachings would increase – it is happening now. Jesus says that natural disasters would escalate – earthquakes, famines, wars and rumours of wars: terrible things – Politicians are crying peace at the same time war is escalating around the world.

What the Spirit said, is being fulfilled now. What Jesus said, is being fulfilled now.

Let's see what the Father said, would happen in the last days. "I will pour out my spirit upon all flesh. And your sons and your daughters shall prophesy, and I shall do great signs and wonders in the earth to bring the heathen in" (Acts 2:17-19). "To give us the unsaved souls (people who do not know Jesus) as our heritage. The uttermost parts of the earth for our habitation" (Psalm 2:8). So now we are starting to see what the Father said, be fulfilled! **We're starting to see a mighty revival.**

Around the world there is a mighty move of the Spirit of God going on. People are getting healed in Malaysia, miracles are happening there. The end of this age is closer than you think! There is Revival up in Europe, there is Revival in Russia, and there is Revival in China. There is Revival in India. Nation after nation is experiencing fresh moves of God. Revival is breaking out all over the world. Before the Rapture it will sweep the earth. We will have Revival because this is what we are crying out for, in Jesus name! Praise God!

Paul in Hebrews 9:28, and in Titus 2:13, gives us the same message. What is God telling us? He's telling us to anticipate the event of His appearing with joyous expectation and preparation. Prepare your hearts so that they are Rapture Ready!

But others (who don't believe in The Rapture) are telling us to prepare for the Tribulation – get your wheelbarrows, stock them up with food, dig underground tunnels and conceal them, fill up your storehouses, get your water purifiers, fill up your 44 gallon drums; we're going to have to run into the mountains, we're going to have to hide. Hardly sounds like a glorious church living in victory, does it?

Luke 21:28, Hebrews 9:28, Titus 2:13, tells us to expect the event, to anticipate the event of His appearing with joyous expectation.

> *"And when these things begin to come to pass, then look up, and lift up your heads; for your redemption draweth nigh"* (Luke 21:28).

> *"So Christ was once offered to bear the sins of many; and unto them that look for him shall he appear the second time without sin unto salvation"* (Hebrews 9:28).

> *"Looking for that blessed hope, and the glorious appearing of the great God and our Saviour Jesus Christ"* (Titus 2:13).

Let's Expect This Event with Great Joy!

When we study the Greek break-down, it tells us it's a joyous expectation. It's a joyous preparation. It's looking forward to Jesus Christ coming with great joy. Not with great fear. Running out into the desert and burying food out there to eat when the world is in famine – there is no joy in that. That's fear!

There are some places in the earth today, where the church is underground. They meet in secret because it is against the law to be a Christian. These believers, even more need to know the victory they have in Christ. The blessing of Abraham and what it means, they need to be praying for their nation and it's leaders to be saved, so that they can live in peace until the Rapture of the Church.

A church that is living in fear is not an overcoming Church. That's not a victorious Church. And that's definitely not the salvation that Jesus Christ bought for us at Calvary.

The salvation that Jesus Christ bought for us at Calvary was a full salvation, *'you shall receive the life of God, you shall receive the joy of God.'* Now if we have to run away and hide because some Anti-Christ is going to come after us with his armies, there would be no great victory in that, would there?

The Anti-Christ is coming in the power by Satan and his authority. We have the authority of our Lord Jesus Christ! The gates of hell themselves cannot prevail against the Church. The devil himself cannot prevail against the Church, standing in the authority and the name of Jesus.

The reason why the Anti-Christ can't be revealed until after the church is Raptured, is because we will bind and break his power, in the name of Jesus. He can't do anything while the Church is here, operating in God's authority.

Some people are saying that the Anti-Christ is going to come on the scene, and we're going to be around for 3½ years of the Anti-Christ's reign and rule, and then in the mid-Tribulation we're all going to disappear. No! We're not going to be around for any of the Anti-Christ's reign and rule. The Bible tells us (in 2 Thessalonians 2:7) that the spirit of iniquity is already at work in the earth, only the force that restrains him will continue to restrain him, until that force or power is taken out of the way. And then the Anti-Christ shall be revealed.

Some people say the restraining force is the Holy Spirit. Or that the Holy Spirit is going to be taken out of the way, so the Anti-Christ can be revealed. I believe the restraining force is the church empowered by the Holy Spirit, through the Word of God, in the Name of Jesus! Jesus says the anointing that we receive abides with us forever. And if we lose the Holy Spirit, we lose our salvation; because He is the agent of salvation.

The Bible says when the Holy Spirit departs from a Church, write "Ichabod" over the door – the Glory of God has departed (1 Samuel 4:21). God is not going to say we can have the Holy Spirit all of our life, and then, just so He can reveal the Anti-Christ, He's going to take the Holy Spirit out of the way, leaving us comfort-less. Who is the Holy Spirit? He is the power of God in the believer, He is our strength, our counsellor, comforter, guide and friend. He is God in you and me and He won't leave us defenceless and at the mercy of the devil and his Anti-Christ. He loves us too much for that to ever happen.

We would be the devil's mincemeat if the Holy Spirit was taken out and we were left behind. Just imagine, we've been binding and breaking the devil's power, getting people born-again for the last 10, 20, 30, 40, 50, 60 years, however long we've been living, until the Holy Spirit is taken out of the way, and suddenly we're left down here. The devil's going to come knocking on our door – he'd come straight to our door and get us. He would say, "I've got you now, you can't bind me any longer, destroy my works for the last 20, 40, 50 years, now I'm going to destroy you"

God is not going to leave us down here at the mercy of the devil, without the power of the Holy Spirit. No! If the Holy Spirit goes, all who are ready will go with Him!

I believe we go, but the Holy Spirit stays. David told us, *"Where do I get away from the presence of God? If I go to the highest heavens, He's there. If I go to the pit, He's there."* God's Spirit is omnipresent. God's Spirit is everywhere. We can't get away from the Holy Spirit.

Not only that, the Bible tells us in the Book of Romans, the Book of Ezekiel, and other Books, that the nation of Israel will be born-again. Paul tells us that the remnant of Israel, the whole nation that is surviving at that time, shall be saved. You can't get saved without the Holy Spirit!

The Holy Spirit has to be here in order for people to be saved during the Tribulation. If the Holy Spirit leaves at the beginning of the Tribulation, that means nobody can be born-again anymore, and that's not the Gospel.

If the Holy Spirit leaves here, at the beginning of the Tribulation, and leaves us behind, the Gospel can't get preached. Because otherwise we would be preaching the Gospel in our strength, and not in His strength.

Jesus says the Gospel will be preached until the very end. The Gospel will be preached in all nations unto the end. And we preach the Gospel through the anointing of the Holy Spirit. The Holy Spirit is not leaving the earth. People who say that have got it all wrong.

It is the Church that is the restraining force. It is the Church empowered by the Holy Spirit that restrains the devil. It is the Church that gets taken out of the way, so the Anti-Christ can be revealed in his time. There is a time allotted for the Anti-Christ to reign and rule. It is a seven year period, known as 'Jacob's Trouble' or 'Daniel's Seventieth Week'. The second half will be much worse than the first half, being known as 'Great Tribulation'.

That is the time allotted to the Anti-Christ to reign and rule, and to work the devil's plan. He can't be revealed until the Church is taken out of the way, because the gates of hell will not prevail against the Church. The spirit of iniquity, the Anti-Christ spirit is already at work, only there is a restraining force. And that is your prayers, and it is the Saints of God's prayers, around the face of this earth! As we pray, we are restraining the devil. That's what we're doing – and we will continue to do that, until we are taken out of the way.

The Bible tells us in the Book of Revelation 11:1-13, that there are two witnesses who preach the Gospel for the second 3½ years of the Tribulation (a period of 1260 days). They get murdered by the Anti-Christ armies, 3½ days before Jesus Christ returns. However, Jesus Christ raises them from the dead. Then they hear a great voice from heaven saying to them, "Come up here!" They then ascend up to heaven in a cloud, and their enemies see this happen. What do you think those two witnesses do while they are on the earth for the second half of the Great Tribulation? They preach the Gospel under the anointing of the Holy Spirit, until they are raptured (as explained above). The Holy Spirit has to be here for those two prophets to preach the Gospel.

I like what Marvin Ford said. He had a heart attack and went to heaven, before David Wilkins raised him from the dead, and he had to come back. He said while he was up there Jesus Christ told him, before He comes with His church, He's coming for His church! But before He comes for His church, He's coming to His church! Hallelujah! So after He's come to His church, and we've experienced a great miracle and healing \revival, which will result in the last great harvest of souls, Jesus will come for us and catch us all away.

So the three things to look for are:
1. Jesus warned us there would be an increase in wars, famines, pestilences and natural disasters. Matthew 24:6,7.

2. The Holy Spirit says we're going to have doctrines of devils, and things that are going to try to seduce people away from the Word, and their relationships with Jesus. 1 Timothy 4:1.

3. And the Father says that in the last days we're going to have Revival. He says the Spirit of God is going to be poured out on all flesh, and that He's going to do signs and wonders. That's what the Father says! Acts 2:17,18,19.

Joel prophesied this and Peter reiterated it in the second chapter of the Book of Acts. 'Watch, in the last days, when you see these things...' We've seen Israel become a nation, we've seen them take Jerusalem, we have seen Jerusalem restored as the capital of Israel. We see the doctrines of devils being spread everywhere. We see the famines and the earthquakes, and now the Coronavirus affecting all the nations of the earth. We are seeing people departing from the faith, however at the same time we are also seeing a mighty Revival. There is a great awakening starting to happen on the face of the earth. These things tell us that this is the very last days, and our redemption draws nigh. Praise God! Jesus is soon to return to this planet. Exciting isn't it?

Chapter Five

THE RAPTURE

Some people get very upset with the word 'Rapture.' They say, Shaun, the word Rapture does not appear in the Bible. So how can you talk about an event that does not appear in the Bible?

In actual fact there are many words, or terminologies, that Christians use today that don't appear in the Bible. Very simply, the word 'demon' for instance, does not appear in the King James version of the Bible. It says 'devil', but you won't find 'demon' in the King James, but we all know there are demons running rampant around the place – till we bind them, by taking authority over them in the name of Jesus.

What we want to know then is, if the word 'Rapture' doesn't appear in the bible, does the truth of the 'Rapture' appear in the Bible. Praise God, it does! The Bible very clearly teaches about a pre-tribulation Rapture of the Church.

There are many confusing voices today in the Christian community about the Rapture, but now as our redemption draws nigh, let's allow the most authoritative and truthful voice of all to speak. Let's look at God's Holy Word, and let's agree to accept exactly what the Scriptures teach.

What does the word Rapture mean? According to the Webster's Dictionary, the word means 'the state of being carried away with joy, love, etc.', 'ecstasy, or an expression of great joy, pleasure.' So then, when people talk about the Rapture, they are referring to the catching up of the church, or the departure of the church, from planet Earth.

> *"For this we say unto you by the word of the Lord, that we which are alive and remain unto the coming of the Lord shall not prevent them which are asleep. (Prevent means go before them which are asleep.) For the Lord Himself shall descend from heaven with a shout, with the voice of the archangel, and with the trump of God: and the dead in Christ shall rise first: Then we which are alive and remain shall be caught up together with them in the clouds, to meet the Lord in the air: and so shall we ever be with the Lord. Wherefore comfort one another with these words"* (1 Thessalonians 4:15-18).

End times should be a time when we can take the Word of God and use it to comfort and encourage one another. No matter what is happening in the world, God is not going to forsake His people.

The Bible says He will NEVER leave us, nor will He forsake us. Some people say that the Church is going to be here during the Tribulation. The Holy Spirit is going to be taken out of the way. Well, if God takes the Holy Spirit out of the way, God has "forsaken" you. The Bible says He will NEVER leave us, nor FORSAKE us (Hebrews 13:5).

The Holy Spirit is the presence of God with us, and if God would take the Holy Spirit and leave us behind, that means God is leaving us, or has left us. God says I will never leave you or forsake you. We are not going to be left behind, we are going to be taken out of the way, before the judgement of God falls. We are going to be caught up, to meet the Lord in the clouds in the air.

The Church is going to depart, and here is where it is found in the Word.

> *"For the Lord Himself shall descend from heaven with a shout, with the voice of the archangel, and with the trump of God: and the dead in Christ shall rise first: Then we which are alive and remain shall be caught up together with them in the clouds, to meet the Lord in the air: and so shall we ever be with the Lord. Wherefore comfort one another with these words"* (1 Thessalonians 4:16-18).

In the presence of the Lord is fullness of joy (Psalm 16:11). So then the church of the Lord Jesus Christ is going to depart from this earth and be caught up (raptured away), to the very presence of Jesus Christ himself to enjoy and experience all of the fullness of his joy that he has for us. WOW! Isn't that something to look forward to?

Chapter Six

Peace and Safety

"But of the times and the seasons, brethren, ye have no need that I write unto you. For yourselves know perfectly that the day of the Lord so cometh as a thief in the night. For when they shall say, Peace and Safety; then sudden destruction cometh upon them, as travail upon a woman with child; and they shall not escape" (1 Thessalonians 5:1-3).

We have two messages here. We have the Church being caught up in the air to meet the Lord. Jesus comes as a thief in the night and takes His church away from the trouble that is to come. It is very comforting to know that we will be caught up and taken away from the time of 'Jacob's Trouble', 'Daniel's Seventieth Week'.

Jesus says, *'listen, you look at the weather and you know when it's going to rain, and when it's going to be fine; but you can't tell the signs of the times'* (Matthew 16:3).

According to the previous verse, the Church is to understand the signs of the times. We are to read what is going on prophetically in the Bible, and know exactly where we are at, in God's timetable of events.

The Bible says that the day of the Lord comes as a thief in the night, for when they say peace and safety, then suddenly destruction comes upon them. It doesn't say it's going to come upon us. Some people say we are going to go through the Tribulation – *'Oh the destruction of God is going to come upon us, 'All this Tribulation, all this testing is just going to pour down on the church, and we're going to have to go through it.'* It says in the Bible it is going to come upon them, those who don't know Jesus or aren't living for Him. Not those who are living for Him, they will be caught up and away from the trouble to come.

We can comfort one another with these words. Now let's proceed from when they say peace and safety. What did they start saying after the Iraqi War? Peace, peace, safety and peace. Listen to what the political leaders of the World are saying. "We've got to have a Peace Treaty, we've got to get around the Peace Table." It's not just the Hippies who are saying 'peace'. It's not just the Greenies who are saying 'peace'. It's the political leaders of the World who are now saying we've got to have 'peace', we've got to have 'safety'. Mainstream media and many others are talking about the possible concerns of nuclear war. Many in our world today are saying, 'we must have peace and get around the negotiating table." The American president, Donald Trump, was working on peace treaties in the Middle East with the nation of Israel.

PEACE AND SAFETY

The political leaders of the world are concerned about the tensions between nations over trade agreements and territorial waters. Some nations are rapidly building up their military and stockpiling missiles and weapons of war. Billions are being spent on new technologies for superior fire power, air power and surveillance, to give one nation the superior edge over another. Yet at the same time, there are peace talks and everyone is saying, "peace and safety!" And the Bible says, suddenly destruction will come upon them.

The nations are preparing for war, while at the same time saying, "peace and safety." The Bible warns that in this time sudden destruction will come upon the nations (1 Thessalonians 5:3).

> *"But ye, brethren, are not in darkness, that that day should overtake you as a thief"* (1 Thessalonians 5:4).

You shouldn't be blind as to when that day's coming.

> *"Ye are all the children of light, and the children of the day: we are not of the night, nor of darkness. Therefore let us not sleep, as do others; but let us watch and be sober"* (1 Thessalonians 5:5-6).

Not walking around looking for Him in the sky, but watching the signs of the times. We're not in the darkness. When we go out there and tell them that Jesus is coming, some people think we have gone nuts or lost our marbles. They are blind to the times, unaware of how close the time is to the fulfilment of these prophecies and the Rapture of the Church.

> *"For they that sleep in the night; and they that be drunken are drunken in the night. But let us, who are of the day be sober, putting on the breastplate of faith and love; and for an helmet, the hope of salvation"* (1 Thessalonians 5:7-8).

We're going to be Raptured, Hallelujah! We're going to be caught up, Praise God. We're going to depart out of this place when destruction comes upon them.

> *"For God hath not appointed us to wrath, but to obtain salvation by our Lord Jesus Christ"* (1 Thessalonians 5:9).

We know that is referring to the Rapture, because He has just said to comfort one another with these words, because we are going to be caught up to meet the Lord in the clouds of the air. Man's best achievements to obtain peace, will always fall short of the mark. Satan comes to steal, kill and destroy. He works through people to achieve this objective. Perfect peace will only be achieved on this earth by the Lord Jesus Christ Himself.

We as the church, are to pray for peace and to bind and restrain the forces of darkness, that are endeavouring to take peace from the earth. We must also pray for a great awakening, revival and salvation of souls, doing our best to reach people with the love and Gospel of Christ. We must do this until the Rapture.

In the presence of the Lord, is the fullness of joy. That's why it says to watch with great expectation, and great joy.

> *"For God hath not appointed us to wrath, but to obtain salvation by our Lord Jesus Christ, who died for us, that, whether we wake or sleep, we should live together with Him. Wherefore comfort yourselves together, and edify one another, even as also ye do. And we beseech you, brethren, to know them which labour among you, and are over you in the Lord, and admonish you; And to esteem them very highly in love for their work's sake. And be at peace among yourselves"* (1 Thessalonians 5:9-13).

That's plain isn't it? It's plain to me anyway: it's as plain as day to me. That's because we're children of the day!

N.B. GOD HAS NOT APPOINTED US TO WRATH!

Chapter Seven

FAITH - THE VITAL INGREDIENT

What does the Rapture mean? What are we talking about when we use the word Rapture? We are talking about the catching up of the Church to meet Jesus Christ in the clouds of the air. It is going to be a day of great joy, Hallelujah! Aren't we going to be happy when we, bow in His physical presence and love on Him? We will then be with our Lord forever!

In the Webster's Dictionary, the word Rapture means to be carried away with great joy, and with great love. Well, I'll tell you what, Jesus is love! It is love that is carrying us away! Great joy and great pleasure. In the arms of Jesus. He's just going to come and carry us away. We're going to be caught up in the clouds to meet the Lord in the air!

Does God have the ability to catch up live human beings? Is God capable of doing this?

Let's establish the fact that a catching up is a Biblical event. Yes, God can catch people up to Himself.

> "And Enoch walked with God after he begat Methuselah three hundred years, and begat sons and daughters: And all the days of Enoch were three hundred sixty and five years: And Enoch walked with God: and he was not; for God took him" (Genesis 5:22-24).

Here is the first Rapture, or catching up, recorded in God's Word. It is in the Book of Genesis, in the Book of Beginnings. God has caught up Enoch, showing us that He is quite capable of catching people up to be with Him.

Why do I know we need faith to be Raptured? Because Enoch needed faith to be Raptured, and if God is not a respecter of persons, if Enoch had to go that way, then you and I will have to go that way.

> "By faith Enoch was translated that he should not see death; and was not found, because God had translated him: for before his translation he had this testimony, that he pleased God" (Hebrews 11:5).

If we want to be Raptured, we'd better have faith for the Rapture, and we'd better have this Testimony, that we please God. Because by faith Enoch was translated that he should not see death, and he was not found because God translated him, and before his translation he had this Testimony, that he pleased God.

> "But without faith it is impossible to please Him: for he that cometh to God must believe that He is, and that He is a rewarder of them that diligently seek Him" (Hebrews 11:6).

FAITH - THE VITAL INGREDIENT

We've got to believe in the promises of God, in order to obtain the promises of God.

How did we get born-again? We got born-again by believing the Word of God, and acting upon it, and receiving Jesus Christ as our Lord and Saviour. And the moment we released faith in that, we were saved.

How did we get filled with the Holy Spirit? Well it just happened to me one day. No! We had to reach out, we had to seek God, we had to hunger for God, we had to believe in the baptism in the Holy Spirit.

Half the church doesn't believe in the baptism in the Holy Spirit. That's why half the church isn't baptised in the Holy Spirit.

But those who believe in it, and ask God, "Father fill me with the Holy Spirit" God fills with the Holy Spirit, and gives to them the ability to speak with other tongues that they may edify themselves.

How did you get it? You got it by faith. By believing in it, by acting on it, and asking God for it. That's how you get healed; that's how you get everything from God. But without faith it is impossible to please Him!

The second Rapture in the Bible is Elijah.

"And it came to pass, when the Lord would take up Elijah into heaven by a whirlwind, that Elijah went

> with Elisha from Gilgal. And Elijah said unto Elisha, Tarry here, I pray thee; for the Lord hath sent me to Bethel. And Elisha said unto him, As the Lord liveth, and as thy soul liveth, I will not leave thee. So they went down to Bethel" (2 Kings 2:1-2).

Out of the mouth of two or three witnesses let every word be established.

> "And it came to pass, as they still went on, and talked, that, behold, there appeared a chariot of fire, and horses of fire, and parted them both asunder; and Elijah went up by a whirlwind into heaven. And Elisha saw it, and he cried, My father, my father, the chariot of Israel, and the horsemen thereof. And he saw him no more: and he took hold of his own clothes, and rent them in two pieces" (2 Kings 2:11-12).

God caught Elijah, physically AND bodily, up into heaven. But Elijah believed that he was going to be Raptured. He told Elisha he was going to leave him that day. He believed God was going to take him. He had faith to be Raptured. He left Gilgal, he was moving, he was going out. And Elijah said unto Elisha *'tarry here I pray thee, for the Lord hath sent me to Bethel.'* And Elisha said unto him, *"As the Lord lives, I will not leave you."* See they both knew! They both were believing that God was going to take Elijah this day. It says in verse 1, *"And it came to pass, when the Lord would take up Elijah."* So obviously they were believing for this. They had a revelation of it. They knew Elijah was going to depart this day.

The third Rapture found in the bible, is none other than the Lord Jesus Christ Himself. (People don't believe in the Rapture – the Bible is full of Raptures. There is none so blind as those who will not see.)

> *"And when He had spoken these things, while they beheld, He was taken up; and a cloud received Him out of their sight"* (Acts 1:9).

He was taken up! The Lord Jesus Christ was taken up! He was Raptured! He was caught up! Call it whatever you like. He left this place, He went up, and a cloud received Him out of their sight."

Jesus Christ then was the third person that we find Raptured in the Word of God.

So then the catching up of live human beings is a proven ability of our God.

Chapter Eight

THE GREAT ESCAPE

We have seen quite clearly that God has the ability to remove live human beings from this earth. The answer to those people who say "What is this Rapture that you're talking about?" Is this, "It is when God catches up His people to Himself." It is very clearly taught in the Book of Thessalonians.

> *"For the Lord Himself shall descend from heaven with a shout, with the voice of the archangel, and with the trump of God: and the dead in Christ shall rise first: Then we which are alive and remain shall be caught up together with them in the clouds, to meet the Lord in the air: and so shall we ever be with the Lord"* (1 Thessalonians 4:16,17).

We will be in His presence forever. And it's going to be a great day of great joy. Hence the word Rapture means, 'to be caught up, to be carried away, with great joy.'

God gives us a mighty promise in the Book of Luke.

> *"Watch ye therefore, and pray always, that ye may be accounted worthy to escape all these things that shall come to pass, and to stand before the Son of man"* (Luke 21:36).

"Watch ye therefore, and pray always, that ye may be accounted worthy to escape all these things" ... how many of them? Half of them? No! ALL of them. None of them? No! ALL of them. The Bible says WATCH YOU THEREFORE.

Now I know that some teachings have us going at the half way point. If people want to go half way, if they want to catch the second bus, that's quite alright with me; but I intend to go in the beginning. My bible promises me that if I will watch and pray always – if I stay in that position of faithfulness to the Lord, if I'm believing for this Rapture, if I'm watching and believing for this event, then it says: *"Pray always, that ye may be counted worthy to escape ALL OF THESE THINGS that shall come to pass, ..."* Not half of them, but all of them. And where shall we be? *"and to stand before the Son of man."*

Jesus Used the Word 'Escape'

The word 'escape' in the Greek, is very interesting. It means to 'flee out of.' It comes from two root words in the Greek, one of them meaning 'a motion or an action that precedes something', and the other root word means 'to vanish away from.'

People don't believe in the Rapture, and yet here we have it. Jesus Christ believes in the Rapture!

It states here *"watch ye therefore, and pray always, that ye may be accounted worthy to escape* (flee out of, to vanish away from) *all these things"*, before these things happen, ALL OF THEM. Before any of these tribulation times that are coming upon the earth happen.

Jesus commands, watch and pray always that you may be counted worthy, that you might be in that position of faithfulness, that you can escape out of, vanish away, from all of these things.

We know the Bible says that in the twinkling of an eye we shall be changed. And the 'twinkling of an eye' comes from the Greek word that we get our word 'atom' from. It means 'in a space that can no further be divided.' We are going to vanish away from all of these things, suddenly. We'll be here one minute, and we'll be gone the next!

> *"Then shall two be in the field; the one shall be taken, and the other left. Two women shall be grinding at the mill; the one shall be taken, and the other left"* (Matthew 24:40,41).

> *"I tell you, in that night there shall be two in the one bed; the one shall be taken, and the other shall be left"* (Luke 17:34).

I asked God if some of these people were lazy. Some working and some sleeping in bed? God said, (God always accounts for everything in His Word) that in different parts of the world, while we are awake other people are asleep. The church of the Lord Jesus Christ is around the face of the whole world, and on that day when Jesus comes, some Christians are going to be asleep in bed, but because they've been faithful and they're standing on the Word of God, they'll be taken. Other Christians will be going about their daily tasks; one will be taken, and the other one left behind.

Two asleep in bed, one taken, one left behind. Two grinding at the mill, one taken, one left behind. God even allows for the difference of night and day in different parts of the earth.

The Scripture says, *"Watch therefore, and pray always, that ye may be accounted worthy to escape ALL of these things."* Not some of them, not half of them, but all of them, that you may vanish away from ... a motion, or an action, that precedes something.

We've seen three Raptures in the Old Covenant. The first one was Enoch in Genesis 5:24. We see that Enoch was the first person to be caught up bodily and alive to the presence of God. We found out in Hebrews 11:5 it was by faith Enoch was translated, that he should not see death.

Elijah was the second person to be caught up, alive and bodily, unto the throne of God. We see that in II Kings 2:11, where Elisha was with him, and the chariot of God swept down, and Elijah was taken up to the presence of God.

The third person to be caught up alive physically into heaven, was none other than the Lord Jesus Christ Himself. The Book of Acts 1:9 tells us that Jesus Christ was caught up alive, into the throne of God.

The fourth rapture will be that of the Church as it is taken by Jesus to escape all that is going to come to pass on this earth during the last seven years of tribulation.

The faithful Church will vanish away and stand before the Son of Man, the Lord Jesus Christ.

> *"After this I looked, and, behold, a door was opened in heaven: and the first voice which I heard was as it were of a trumpet talking with me; which said, Come up hither, and I will shew thee things which must be hereafter. And immediately I was in the spirit: and, behold, a throne was set in heaven, and one sat on the throne"* (Revelation 4:1,2).

Revelation Four starts with the words 'After this.' After what? After God finishes dealing with the Church in the Earth, the vision moves to Heaven and the Throne of God. Why, because the Rapture marks the end of the Church age. Hence the door opened in Heaven. The Church will pass from this earth through the door and into the presence of God. John will go on in Chapters four and five of Revelation to describe the Church worshiping before the Throne before Jesus takes the book from his Father's hand. He then proceeds to undo the first seal, which releases the Anti-Christ on the earth (the rider on the white horse of Revelation Chapter Six) to fulfil his mission until his ultimate destruction at the Hand of Christ at the Battle of Armageddon.

In Revelation Chapter 1, Jesus Christ is revealed as the King of Kings, and Lord of Lords. The Apostle John fell down as dead at His feet, yet he'd lived with Jesus three years, he'd travelled around that part of the world with Jesus for three years. He was known as the Apostle that Jesus loved.

John first of all had a revelation of Jesus Christ the Son of Man, then he had a revelation of Jesus Christ as the Good Shepherd. Then he had a revelation of Jesus Christ as the Lamb of God. Then he had a revelation of Jesus Christ as Head of the Church. John had those revelations. He knew Him as the Lord and Saviour who had risen from the dead. He had communed with Jesus, worked miracles in His Name.

Now, John in the Book of Revelation, Rev 1:13-17, when he sees Jesus says: *"And I saw one like unto the son of man."* Did he think, I know Jesus, I know Him as the son of man, I've eaten at the same table as Him, I've known Him as the head of the Church but who is this, that I'm seeing now? I know Jesus, but I have never seen him revealed like this before. Then he starts to explain what he sees, the Lord God, Jesus Christ, in all of His magnificence and glory.

And he sees Jesus Christ, as King of Kings, and Lord of Lords, the Alpha and Omega. And when he sees Jesus Christ in His magnificence, His glorified state, His eyes like flames of fire, His hair like wool, and His feet like burnished brass, and as he sees Jesus Christ in all of His glory, and the magnificence, and awesomeness, of this vision, as he stands before Him; John just falls at His feet like he's dead.

John the apostle knows Jesus, yet he says: *"I see one like unto the Son of Man"*, and he falls down at Jesus' feet as dead, because all of the spirit that is in John, has just totally departed from him. He is undone and now out of fear he just falls down at Jesus' feet, totally paralysed by fear at the awesome sight of the risen King of Kings, and Lord of Lords.

And the first thing Jesus says, as He reaches over and touches him on the shoulder, (I just love this), is *"John, fear not..."*

John probably thinks, man, "it is Jesus." Then Jesus starts to tell him, *"I am He that was, and was dead, and now I am alive forevermore."* And Jesus starts to reveal himself as King of Kings, and Lord of Lords. The Almighty.

In Chapter Two and Three of Revelation, Jesus Christ, by the Holy Spirit, starts to bring a teaching through John, to the Church. He starts to put things in order. He takes the seven churches which are representative of the Body of Christ in the world of today, and one by one he starts to commend them for the things that they are doing right, and He starts to rebuke them for the things that need to be put in order. He covers all of these things, all the way down to the end of Chapter Three.

> *"He that hath an ear, let him hear what the Spirit saith unto the churches"* (Revelation Chapter 3:22).

These are not the days to grow weary in well doing! These are the days to get on fire for Jesus! Return to our first love, do the work that we did when we were so keen and just born again. Stay faithful and stay in fellowship for that day, "that

Great day" will soon be upon us and the faithful Church will be gone, caught up to the throne of God. Seated with Christ in heavenly places.

John starts to describe this incredible sight that he sees before the throne. We'll pick it up again at:

> *"And I saw in the right hand of him that sat on the throne a book written within and on the back side, sealed with seven seals. And I saw a strong angel proclaiming with a loud voice, who is worthy to open the book, and to loose the seals thereof?*
>
> *And no man in heaven, nor in earth, neither under the earth, was able to open the book, neither to look thereon. And I wept much, because no man was found worthy to open and to read the book, neither to look thereon.*
>
> *And one of the elders saith unto me, Weep not: behold, The Lion of the tribe of Judah, the root of David, hath prevailed to open the book ... (Who? Jesus) ... and to loose the seven seals thereof.*
>
> *And I beheld, and, lo, in the midst of the throne and of the four beasts, and in the midst of the elders, stood a Lamb as it had been slain, having seven horns and seven eyes, which are the seven Spirits of God sent forth into all the earth.*

And he came and took the book out of the right hand of Him that sat upon the throne.

And when he had taken the book, the four beasts and four and twenty elders fell down before the Lamb, having every one of them harps, and golden vials full of odours, which are the prayers of saints.

And they sung a new song, ... (Now watch the song that they sing) ... saying, Thou art worthy to take the book, and to open the seals thereof: for thou was slain, and has redeemed us to God by thy blood out of every kindred, and tongue, and people, and nation;

And hast made us unto our God kings and priests: and we shall reign on the earth" (Revelation 5:1-10).

That is the Church there. Raptured up, after God has finished dealing with the Church on the earth, the Church is taken up.

Jesus says:
> *"Watch ye therefore, and pray always, that ye may be accounted worthy to escape all these things that shall come to pass, and to stand before the Son of man"* (Luke 21:36).

As Jesus Christ takes the book out of the hand of His father, the Church of the Lord Jesus Christ, the Redeemed of the Lord, who have been purchased by the blood of Jesus and raptured to heaven from this earth, fall down and we worship Him, and sing a new song, "thou art worthy to take the book, and to open the seals thereof, for thou was slain, and has redeemed us to God."

The faithful Church are kings and priests unto God and they will reign on the earth with Jesus Christ when they return with him from glory, where we will be for seven years while the great tribulation (the time of God's judgement) takes place on earth.

Chapter Nine

THE CHURCH BEFORE THE THRONE

When Jesus Christ has finished dealing with His Church on the earth, something is going to happen. When the time of the Gentiles is fulfilled, the Rapture of the Church will take place, and God will start dealing again with the nation of Israel.

> *"After this (after what? After God has finished dealing with his Church on the earth) I looked and, behold, a door was opened in heaven: and the first voice which I heard was as it were of a trumpet talking with me; which said, Come up hither, and I will shew thee things which must be hereafter. And immediately I was in the spirit: and behold, a throne was set in heaven, and one sat on the throne"* (Revelation 4:1).

And so John is taken up in the spirit into heaven. God finishes dealing with the Church on the earth, and John is transported 2000 years into the future, and he starts to describe a scene that he sees in heaven. And this is what he sees:

After God has finished dealing with the Church on the earth, the Church is Raptured to the presence of God. So, John goes through this door, and he says:

> "And immediately I was in the spirit: and, behold, a throne was set in heaven, and one sat on the throne. And he that sat was to look upon like a jasper and a sardine stone: and there was a rainbow round about the throne, in sight like unto an emerald. And round about the throne were four and twenty seats: and upon the seats I saw four and twenty elders sitting, clothed in white raiment: and they had on their heads crowns of gold. And out of the throne proceeded lightnings and thunderings and voices: and there were seven lamps of fire burning before the throne, which are the seven Spirits of God" (Revelation 4:2-6).

(That's a multiplicity of the Holy Spirit.)

> "And before the throne there was a sea of glass like unto crystal: and in the midst of the throne, and round about the throne, were four beasts full of eyes before and behind" (Revelation 4:6).

N.B. Revelation Chapters two and three are the last two thousand years of Church history and God dealing with the Church in the earth.

Revelation Chapters four and five, the Church is in heaven, stands before the throne and Jesus appears before his Church and the Father as the King of Kings, Lord of Glory and Saviour of mankind.

While the Church is in Glory before the throne of the Lord God, Revelation chapter six starts to unfold on the earth. First the Anti-Christ is revealed and starts his move for world dictatorship, as his plan unfolds, God's judgements are poured out culminating with the battle of Armageddon and the return of Christ and His church to this planet to set up his everlasting sign of righteousness.

What is the Church redeemed by? We are redeemed by the blood of Jesus.

Where does the Church come from? The Church comes from every kindred, it comes from every kind of language, it comes from every kind of people, and it comes from every nation.

Wherever they have received Jesus Christ as their Lord and Saviour; doesn't matter what country they live in, what colour their skin is, what language they speak. On that day they will stand before the Son of man!

And the Bible says *"has made us unto God kings and priests: and we shall reign on the earth."* Who's going to reign on the earth? The Redeemed of the Lord. The Church of the Lord Jesus Christ is going to reign and rule. It is a promise of God that we shall reign on the earth.

Now the reason why the Bible says, *"and we shall reign on the earth"*, is because at this point in time, the Church is in heaven, standing before the throne of God.

John describes this scene:

> "And I beheld, and I heard the voice of many angels round about the throne and the beasts and the elders: ... (listen to how many there were) ... and the number of them was ten thousand times ten thousand, and thousands of thousands;" (Revelation 5:11).

> Verses 12-14 *"Saying with a loud voice, worthy is the Lamb that was slain to receive power, and riches, and wisdom, and strength, and honour, and glory, and blessing.*

> *And every creature which is in heaven, and on earth, and under the earth, and such as are in the sea, and all that are in them, heard I saying, Blessing, and honour, and glory, and power, be unto Him that sitteth upon the throne, and unto the Lamb for ever and ever.*

> *And the four beasts said, Amen. And the four and twenty elders fell down and worshipped Him that liveth for ever and ever."*

Now the four and twenty elders are the representation of the whole of the Church of the Lord Jesus Christ. The Redeemed of the Lord out of the nation of Israel, plus the Redeemed of the Lord out of the Gentile nations of the earth.

They are the representation of the whole of the Church. John describes how many there are: ten thousand times ten thousand, and thousands of thousands.

Where did they come from? He tells us in verse 9. *"...We have been redeemed by the blood of Jesus out of every kindred, and tongue, and people, and nation."*

N.B. The reason that the 24 elders are only a representation of the whole church and not the whole church is because many people are yet to be saved on earth during the tribulation and added to their number still in the future.

We've been made kings and priests unto God. We are to reign and rule in life now, by the Spirit of God and in the authority of the Name of Jesus. We are to take authority over Satan, binding His power and the influence of the kingdom of darkness. We reign now until we are raptured, as the restraining force. Then when Jesus returns at His second coming, we will return with Him and we shall reign and rule under Him for a thousand years.

What shall we do? We shall reign on the earth. That's when Jesus returns. We shall return with Him and reign on the earth.

The church will then be complete. A combination of all those saved in Old Testament times, plus all those saved in New Testament plus all those saved during the tribulation time. We will all be together and reigning with Jesus on earth during the millennium.

Chapter Ten

RAPTURES FIVE, SIX AND SEVEN

People preaching theologies argue, "is there going to be a Rapture of the Church?" Is this possible? Well don't ever forget, "all things are possible to him who believes" (Mark 9:23).

But in fact there are seven Raptures recorded in God's Word. We have looked at the first four:

1. Enoch Genesis 5:22-24
2. Elijah 2 Kings 2:11-12
3. The Lord Jesus Acts 1:9
4. The Church Revelations 4:1-2, 1 Thessalonians 4:16-17

Now we will look at the Fifth, Sixth and Seventh Raptures contained in the Bible.

> Revelation 7:9-17 says, *"After this I beheld, and, lo, a great multitude, which no man could number, of all nations, and kindreds, and people, and tongues,*

stood before the throne, and before the Lamb, clothed with white robes, and palms in their hands; And cried with a loud voice, saying, Salvation to our God which sitteth upon the throne, and unto the Lamb.

And all the angels stood round about the throne, and about the elders and the four beasts, and fell before the throne on their faces, and worshipped God, Saying, Amen: Blessing, and glory, and wisdom, and thanksgiving, and honour, and power, and might, be unto our God for ever and ever. Amen.

And one of the elders answered, saying unto me, What are these which are arrayed in white robes? And whence came they?

And I said unto him, Sir, thou knowest. And he said to me, These are they which came out of great tribulation, and have washed their robes, and made them white in the blood of the Lamb.

Therefore are they before the throne of God, and serve Him day and night in His temple: and He that sitteth on the throne shall dwell among them.

They shall hunger no more, neither thirst any more; neither shall the sun light on them, nor any heat.

For the Lamb which is in the midst of the throne shall feed them, and shall lead them unto living fountains of waters: and God shall wipe away all tears from their eyes."

That is the fifth Rapture, and it is the mid-Tribulation Rapture of the Saints.

A lot of people think that even after the Church is gone, the devil is going to have it all his own way. Well, it's not true.

God never ever leaves Himself without a witness, and God anoints 144,000 male Jewish virgins, and they're sealed with the seal of God. For the first 3½ years, to 4 years, they go around the earth preaching the Gospel of the Lord Jesus Christ, and people get born-again during the Tribulation period.

Also, there will be a lot of back-slidden Christians, who will wake up one day, or they'll be driving their cars, and their partners, or passengers, will disappear. Or they'll be sitting in church listening to the preacher, and the preacher will go, and most of the Church, and they'll think "oh dear, I've missed the Rapture", and they will get on their hands and knees and they will repent.

They will have to go through the first half of the Tribulation, but there will be a mid-Tribulation Rapture of the Saints, and that is what we have just read here. These are they that have come out of great tribulation.

This Rapture takes place approximately 3½ years into the last 7 years of this world's time as we know it.

The sixth Rapture in the bible, is the Rapture of the 144,000 Jewish evangelists.

> Revelation 14:1-3 says, *"And I looked, and, lo, a Lamb stood on the mount Zion, and with Him an hundred forty and four thousand, having His Father's name written in their foreheads.*
>
> *And I heard a voice from heaven, as the voice of many waters, and as the voice of a great thunder: and I heard the voice of harpers harping with their harps:*
>
> *And they sung as it were a new song before the throne, and before the four beasts, and the elders: and no man could learn that song but the hundred and forty and four thousand, which were redeemed from the earth."*

Where did they come from? They're before the throne of God. They came from the earth. Revelation 14:4 *"These are they which were not defiled with women; for they are virgins..."*

What do they do? Revelation 14:4 *"...These are they which follow the Lamb whithersoever He goeth..."*

A person once asked me, 'How do you know the 144,000 preached the Gospel?' I said, 'Because my Bible tells me they followed the Lamb, and you can't follow Jesus without preaching the Gospel.'

Followers of the Lamb are a witness to God. And the Bible says *"You shall be filled with the Holy Ghost, and with the power."* Why? *"That you may witness for Me, both in Jerusalem, Judea, Samaria, and unto the uttermost parts of the earth."* So the 144,000 preach the Gospel and follow the teaching of our Lord Jesus Christ the Lamb of God.

Who are they? They are male, Jewish, virgins. They are the first fruits. "These are they which were not defiled with women; for they are virgins. These were redeemed from among men, being the first fruits unto God and to the Lamb."

Let's get things in verse context, chapter context, and covenant context.

Jesus Christ is referred to as the first fruits. The Church is referred to as the first fruits. And the 144,000 are referred to as the first fruits. So how do you know which are the first fruits then?

It's easy. Jesus Christ was a first fruit – He was the first born from the dead. He said, I am He that was alive and was dead, but now I am alive for evermore, Amen! He paid the price. He was crucified, He died, and went to Hell, but God by the power of the Holy Spirit, rose Jesus from the dead, and He was the first fruits unto God. First to rise from spiritual death (Hell). (Hebrews 1:6).

Then we gave our lives to Jesus; and we became God's first fruits. Taken from the Kingdom of darkness translated to the Kingdom of light.

After the Church is taken out of the earth, and this world reverts back to Jewish time (that's how I like to refer to it) for the last 7 years of Daniel's prophecy, then these 144,000 are the first Jews to get born-again of that time frame.

They are young men who get a hold of the fact that Jesus Christ is the Messiah. They give their lives to Jesus, and for the first 3½ years they go around preaching the Gospel. They are sealed with a seal that no man can harm them. God supernaturally protects them and they travel through the earth preaching the Gospel, because God never lets the Anti-Christ nor the devil have his own way.

When the Anti-Christ is rising to power, and while he is condemning religions and righteousness and morality, condemning Christianity, and the Jewish religion, God has these 144,000 male, Jewish, virgins following the Lord Jesus Christ, preaching the Gospel.

They are the firstfruits out of that time of Daniel's last week.

Somewhere in the mid-Tribulation time, to slightly after mid-Tribulation, (I like to place it about 3½ years into Tribulation), they get redeemed from the earth, and they stand before the Son of Man.

They are the sixth Rapture in the Bible.

Revelation 14:5 says, *"And in their mouth was found no guile: for they are without fault before the throne of God."*

The seventh Rapture in the Bible is found in revelation Chapter 11 Verse 12. The seventh Rapture is the Rapture of the two witnesses. (I believe a strong possibility for the two witnesses to be Enoch and Elijah, but that will be explained in a later book.)

Revelation 11:12 says, *"And they heard a great voice from heaven saying unto them, Come up hither. And they ascended up to heaven in a cloud; and their enemies beheld them."*

God never leaves Himself without a witness. After God takes the 144,000 out of the earth, somewhere between mid-Tribulation and four years, (the mid-Tribulation Rapture of the saints has taken place, the 144,000 are now gone), these two witnesses preach the Gospel in the streets of Jerusalem for the last 3½ year of Daniel's 70th week.

They are a real thorn in the side of the Anti-Christ.

At this point in time the Anti-Christ has broken his covenant with the nation of Israel, he has betrayed his covenant agreement with them, which was to be 7 years of peace. He has marched into the temple, and proclaimed himself as God and is backed up by the false prophet.

During this time, the new world order of the day, will have a new 'One-World Religion'.

The Anti-Christ, three and a half years into this last seven years will break his covenant agreement with Israel and the new-world religion, by declaring himself **"God"**.

The Bible says he will speak great blasphemies against the real God. Backed by the False Prophet, he will force everyone to worship him and take his number 666.

After the true Church of the Lord Jesus Christ is Raptured, the New Age Movement, together with a combination of all religions that are left behind, will come right to the forefront. The false prophet will then emerge as the leader of this New Church Movement or Order. It will totally give its allegiance to the Anti-Christ.

The World Council of Churches, and the different established churches around the earth, no matter what or who they are, the ones that are left behind, the ones which have departed from the truth of God's Word, will throw their lot in with the New Church Order. Doctrines like "there are many ways to God, and we have all got this Christ-consciousness." "Get in tune with the universe." "The universe will deliver blessings to you." There could even be a "UFO, alien" deception and doctrine added into the mix. The False Prophet will be the head of this, one world unified church or Whore Church of Revelations 17.

For the first 3½ years the Anti-Christ permits this new Super Church to spread its doctrines around the earth, and he permits worship of their gods. But after 3½ years the Anti-Christ marches into Jerusalem, and he goes into the temple that has been reconstructed, and says 'I am God.'

And the New World Church and all remaining religions or sects of enlightenment will say, 'hang on, we believe we've all got this Christ-consciousness'. Some may refer to this as a universe God mindset.

However, the false prophet (who is the head of the Whore Church, an amalgamation of all false religions) will say, 'now listen, here is God (referring to the Anti-Christ), and everybody must worship him.' The False Prophet will back up his claim with lying signs and wonders. (2 Thessalonians 2:9).

N.B. The author believes that the Whore Church spoken of in Revelation will be an amalgamation of all religions, after the rapture. The churches left behind, established religions and New Age Movement, and any sect that rejects the Lordship of Jesus Christ will eventually unite. Those who do not believe Him to be the one and only true God, will unite to form a Unified World Church. Accepting all doctrinal creeds and stating there are many roads to God and you are free to choose the one that suits you best. Whereas to the Christian, Jesus Christ is the only way to the Father. Those that come to God must come through Jesus Christ (Acts 4:2).

At this point, three and a half years into the last seven years, the whore church (One World Church) will panic and say, 'wait a minute, this doesn't even fit our doctrine'. This is when the Anti-Christ destroys the whore church and outlaws all religion and worship, except the worship of himself alone.

> 2 Thessalonians 2:4 says, *"Who opposes and exalts himself above all that is called God or that is worshipped, so that he sits as God in the temple of God, showing himself that he is God."*

At this point the false prophet erects an image of the Anti-Christ in Jerusalem and people are forced to bow down and worship the Anti-Christ image and have his number forced on them, 666 (Revelation 13:15-18).

N.B. Many End Time Bible students now believe that this numbering of 666 will be in the form of computer coding without which no person will be able to buy or sell as it states in Revelations Chapter 13. This computer chip could be implemented in a person's forehead or just under the skin like the palm of the hand. Already there are trials in place, where people are being numbered and coded in this way so they can be easily traced.

A computer or Google search will reveal the advances that are being made in this technology. There is much talk in our world today of a digital passport, combining with health records and even banking facilities, that may shortly come to being in our society. There are tech companies that are joining forces with vaccine producing companies and even banking businesses, that are desiring these type of systems to be implemented into our world.

Most central banks are looking at CBDCs, which are digital currencies based on block-chain technology. This, together with AI and tracing capabilities of modern technology, means your whereabouts could be known at all times. It would be possible then, for a future world government to implement a 666 system, where people would not be able to trade, buy or sell and do business without participating in the system.

Once again, many companies of the world are developing this type of technology around body data and new financial systems and 5G technology to make our world a more smoother running and technological advanced society. A Google search revealed that Microsoft even registered a patent 2020 060606 for a new type of cryptocurrency system using body activity data. *N. B. refer to page 254.*

After the rapture of the church it will be easy for a world government headed by the Anti-Christ to introduce his 666 number/mark, as the modern technology that never existed before, but now does, will facilitate this.

The bible teaches in the Book of Revelation there is a whore church that is destroyed by the Anti-Christ. The Bible says the Anti-Christ won't permit worship of any kind of religion, or any kind of God.

For 3½ years he will use the New Church Order (whore church) until he betrays it. The false prophet says the Anti-Christ is God, and the false prophet sets up an image of the beast, and he says, 'worship the image of the beast or be executed.'

At this point in time, the Anti-Christ identity is unknown and will be concealed until after the catching away of the church.

> *" He causes all, both small and great, rich and poor, free and slave, to receive a mark on their right hand or on their foreheads, and that no one may buy or sell*

except one who has the mark or the name of the beast, or the number of his name. Here is wisdom. Let him who has understanding calculate the number of the beast, for it is the number of a man: His number is 666" (Revelation 13:16-18).

God is Never Without a Witness!

God has two witnesses on the streets of Jerusalem, and for the last 3½ years they walk up and down the streets of Jerusalem, saying 'Jesus Christ is God, Jesus Christ is God, this man is a liar.' Every time the Anti-Christ sends out his armies against the two witnesses, these armies are destroyed (Revelations 11:5).

Then 3½ days before the mighty return of the Lord Jesus Christ, at His second coming, when He returns with the Church to take possession of the earth, the Anti-Christ kills the two witnesses. He actually kills them!

For 3½ years, the two witnesses have been saying, 'Jesus is coming back. God is more powerful than the Anti-Christ. Repent, give your life to Jesus.' These two have been a thorn in the flesh of the Anti-Christ. What happens when they are killed?

> Revelation 11:8 says, *"and their dead bodies shall lie in the street of the great city, which spiritually is called Sodom and Egypt, where also our Lord was crucified."*

That's Jerusalem. Spiritually called Sodom and Egypt! Why? Because Jerusalem becomes the habitation of every foul demon spirit, every occult practice, because that's where the Anti-Christ sets up his headquarters.

> Revelation 11:9 says, *"And they of the people and kindreds and tongues and nations shall see their dead bodies* (Who? The two witnesses) *three days and an half, and shall not suffer their dead bodies to be put in graves."*

The Anti-Christ gets the world's cameras, news outlets, social media which will go viral round the whole world. *'I have overcome these two witnesses who said Jehovah was God – see I'm more powerful than Jehovah.'* And everyone has a party, and they start sending presents to one another – hallelujah, the Anti-Christ has overcome and is better than God, look the Anti-Christ is more powerful than Jesus Christ. The Anti-Christ has overcome the two witnesses.

> Revelation 11:10 says, *"And they that dwell upon the earth shall rejoice over them, and make merry, and shall send gifts one to another; because these two prophets tormented them that dwelt on the earth."*

Why? Because they kept preaching the Gospel, and warning of the great impending judgement of God. God is never without a witness. For the last 3½ years they preached the Gospel, telling people to repent of their evil ways and that Jesus Christ is coming again.

> Revelation 11:11 says, *"And after three days and a half the Spirit of life from God entered into them, and they stood upon their feet; and great fear fell upon them which saw them."*

Now you can just imagine the fear that falls on earth. These two prophets arise up to life again. Everyone has been throwing parties over their death. Rejoicing and making merry, saying "Sin is great. We finally got rid of every single Christian witness. We finally got rid of every single witness of Jehovah and Jesus Christ. The Anti-Christ is God." And then suddenly these two witnesses come back to life and they stand up on their feet. *"...and great fear fell upon them which saw them"* (Revelation 11:11). This would be beamed all over the world by satellite and social media!

> Revelation 11:12 says, *"And they heard a great voice from heaven saying unto them, Come up hither. And they ascended up to heaven in a cloud; and their enemies beheld them."*

These two witnesses have been preaching the lordship of Jesus. They have been reminding the Anti-Christ that he is not God, telling him nor is his mentor, the devil. They have been reminding the Anti-Christ that Jesus is the soon returning King and that his days are numbered. Then as if by a miracle, the Anti-Christ overcomes these prophets and kills them. They lay dead in the streets for 3½ days. They then miraculously rise from the dead and are raptured, caught up into heaven.

Revelation 11:13 says, *"and the same hour was there a great earthquake, and the tenth part of the city fell, and in the earthquake were slain of men seven thousand: and the remnant were affrighted, and gave glory to the God of heaven."*

I tell you what, some of them really start repenting then! For this is right now at the very, very, last hour when the Lord Jesus Christ will return like lightning, and every eye shall see Him and He will come back with all of His Church.

Praise God, if you have made Jesus the Lord of your life and been living for Him you will return with Him to reign and rule. All the angels will return with Jesus as well. We will watch and rejoice as Jesus takes possession of this earth.

This is the last Rapture in the Bible. The two witnesses being taken up.

So there are seven Raptures recorded in God's Word. Seven Raptures!

There are three Raptures before the Church – Enoch, Elijah and Jesus.

There are three raptures after the Church is taken – mid-Tribulation of the saints, 144,000 Jewish virgins and then the two witnesses.

The Church then is the middle Rapture. Praise God! God has positioned the Church as the middle Rapture. God shows us seven Raptures in the Bible – the number seven being God's number of perfection, or God's number of completion. That which is perfect!

Doesn't it seem strange that God would take all of these other groups – we see a mid-Tribulation Rapture of the saints, we see the 144,000, we see the two witnesses, all taken out of the Tribulation. We see Elijah, we see Enoch, and we see Jesus. Yet misinformed people say, 'I don't believe God is going to take the Church.'

Chapter Eleven

RAPTURE EXPLAINED

The Rapture takes place before the Tribulation. The second advent or the second coming of the Lord Jesus Christ takes place at the end of the Tribulation. There is a difference!

At the Rapture of the church, Jesus' feet do not touch the ground. He comes back in the clouds of glory, the Church is caught up to Jesus, and we return to heaven with Him. We escape all of what's going to happen on the earth during the time of God's judgement. We stand before the Son of Man. We watch Him undo the scroll. We watch Him unveil the seven seals; we see Jesus take the book from the Father. We see Him loose the first seal (Revelation 6), and we see the release of the Anti-Christ. We see how the Anti-Christ is revealed, and is manifest in the earth.

"Now we beseech you, brethren, by the coming of our Lord Jesus Christ, and by our gathering together unto Him" (2 Thessalonians 2:1).

There are two events spoken of in this verse. The first one is the coming of the Lord Jesus Christ. That is when Jesus returns to take possession of the earth at the end of the seven years of Tribulation.

It culminates with the battle of Armageddon – Jesus Christ wins, Amen! He takes possession of the earth. He puts His foot down on the top of that mountain, it splits in half and a river gushes forth from its base and flows down into the Dead Sea, brings life to the Dead Sea, fishes live again in the Dead Sea, and it flows past Jerusalem. Jerusalem becomes a sea port, and flows out this new river into the Mediterranean. There is a new river birthed when Jesus puts His foot on that mountain. That is at the Second Coming.

Zechariah 14:4-9 says,

> *"And his feet shall stand in that day upon the mount of Olives, which is before Jerusalem on the east, and the mount of Olives shall cleave in the midst thereof toward the east and toward the west, and there shall be a very great valley; and half of the mountain shall remove toward the north, and half of it toward the south.*
>
> *And ye shall flee to the valley of the mountains; for the valley of the mountains shall reach unto Azal: yea, ye shall flee, like as ye fled from before the earthquake in the days of Uzziah king of Judah: and the Lord my God shall come, and all the saints with thee.*

> *And it shall come to pass in that day, that the light shall not be clear, nor dark:*
>
> *But it shall be one day which shall be known to the Lord, not day, nor night: but it shall come to pass, that at evening time it shall be light.*
>
> *And it shall be in that day, that living waters shall go out from Jerusalem; half of them toward the former sea, and half of them toward the hinder sea: in summer and in winter shall it be."*
>
> *And the Lord shall be king over all the earth: in that day shall there be one Lord, and his name one.*

But the other event is the Rapture. That's the one you and I go in! *"...and by our gathering together unto Him,..."* Paul is trying to teach the Thessalonians something; he is trying to straighten out something for them. He says:

> *"That ye be not soon shaken in mind, or be troubled, neither by spirit, nor by word, nor by letter as from us, as that the day of Christ is at hand"* (2 Thessalonians 2:2).

There is nothing new under the sun. The same deceiving devils that are trying to tell us today there is no Rapture, that we've got to go through the Tribulation, were working in Paul's day. The Thessalonians were becoming shaken in mind, they were becoming confused, and troubled in spirit.

They questioned if they had missed out on the Rapture, or was there going to be a Rapture, or did they have to go through the Tribulation time, and wait for Jesus to return.

You have to remember they were starting to see the prophecy of Luke 21 totally fulfilled when Jesus predicted the destruction of the temple by the Roman armies, that were encompassing the Holy Land. This happened in 70 AD, but the Gospel had to be preached in all the world for a witness before the end would come.

> *"And this gospel of the kingdom will be preached in all the world as a witness to all the nations, and then the end will come"* (Matthew 24:14).

The above prophecy has now been fulfilled, allowing for the end to come!

Questions were being asked of the Apostle Paul and he addressed these questions in Thessalonians. Followers of Christ were starting to doubt and even get thoughts like, "maybe we have missed the Rapture and the day of destruction is at hand."

Paul says, *"Now we beseech you, brethren, by the coming of our Lord Jesus Christ..."* (that's the second coming of Jesus), *"and by our gathering together unto Him..."* (that's the Rapture of the Church), *"That ye be not soon shaken in mind, or be troubled, neither by spirit, nor by word, nor by letter as from us, as that the day of Christ is at hand."*

He is saying, 'Now listen Church, I want to tell you, don't let people confuse you with this. The day of Christ can't come until something happens first.'

> *"Let no man deceive you by any means: for that day shall not come, except, there come a falling away first,..."* (2 Thessalonians 2:3).

Now I know that most theologians translate this as apostasy, and backsliding from the Lord Jesus Christ, but I believe that is an incorrect translation. It does not hold up in Chapter context. If you study the Chapter here, Paul is not talking about backsliding, he's talking about Jesus coming back, and he's talking about our gathering together unto Him.

In 1 Thessalonians Chapter 4, he has already said Jesus is going to come back and catch us up.

In Chapter 5 he's told us that Jesus hasn't appointed us unto wrath. He said destruction is going to come upon them but we are going to obtain salvation. We haven't been appointed unto wrath. He says when they say peace and safety, suddenly destruction will come upon them, and they won't escape. (1 Thessalonians 5:3)

Jesus tells us in Luke 21:36, that if we watch and pray, then we will escape all of the things that will come. We will escape the destruction. He says, they won't escape, but we the children of light will! Because we are not blind to these things! Jesus is coming like a thief in the night, but, He says, that it doesn't have to be that way for His people, because the Church understands the times and the seasons.

> *"Now we beseech you, brethren, by the coming of our Lord Jesus Christ, and by our gathering together unto Him"* (2 Thessalonians 2:1).

Don't get upset that you've missed out on the Rapture. Don't get upset that someone said there isn't a Rapture. Don't get upset that the day of Christ is at hand.

> *"Let no man deceive you by any means: for that day shall not come, except there come a falling away first..."* (2 Thessalonians 2:3).

In the Greek, that word 'falling away' comes from the word 'apostasia', and it can be translated apostasy, (and most Bible translators translate it that way because they have this mental idea that God is going to beat up the Church), but another correct translation of that word, is the word 'separation.'

So we have to study the Chapter to see which is the most correct translation. The Amplified Bible has a footnote which says a possible rendering of 'apostasy', or 'apostasia', means the departure of the Church. And so it is possible – it is not incorrect – in the Greek language to interpret this Scripture this way. It can be correctly translated in the Greek this way – 'the departure of the Church.'

The Kenneth Weiss translation of the Bible is probably one of the best translations of this verse, and it says, "that day will not come until the departure of the Church takes place first."

The following is a list of other Bible Theologians and commentaries that use the word departure.
- Coverdale (1535)
- Thomas Cranmer (1539)
- Rev. J.R. Major, Ma. (1831)
- John James, L.L.D. (1825)
- Rolent Baher, Breeches Bible (1615)
- John Parkhurst (1851) Lexicon, London
- Properly, a departure.

Let's study this Chapter to see if this Chapter holds up the departure of the Church, or if it is talking about apostasy in a backsliding sense.

"Let no man deceive you by any means: for that day shall not come, except..." (and I'm going to put it this way) a departure of the Church takes place first, and that man of sin be revealed, the son of perdition;"

Now I put it to you. The Anti-Christ cannot be revealed until the Church is taken out of the way. Because Jesus says the gates of hell will not prevail against the Church. *"You shall cast out the devil in My name."* And if we can cast out devils, then a man possessed by devils shouldn't be any worries to the informed and empowered Church. Some people get frightened about this Anti-Christ. Why? He's only empowered by Satan, and Satan is under our feet.

The Anti-Christ is Satan's master play. He's his trump card (if you're a card player) – it's the best he's got. He is not going to play his trump card until he knows all the aces are down. And he's not going to show his best hand until the Church is gone. When the Church is taken out of the way, then he's going to reveal his master plan and his Anti-Christ to become world dictator, otherwise we would bind him if he appeared on the scene right now.

Some people say the Anti-Christ is this one, that one, he's somebody else. His identity is hidden in the Scriptures. We won't know his identity until one day when we're up in heaven, Jesus takes off the seal, and the Anti-Christ hops on his horse and rides it (not that he's on a horse, that is just an analogy of how he is an imitation of Christ), and we look down from heaven and say, 'oh, that's who he is.'

N.B. The number of the beast or Anti-Christ is 666.

"Let no man deceive you by any means: for that day shall not come, except a departure of the Church takes place first, and that man of sin be revealed, the son of perdition;" (2 Thessalonians 2:3).

Look what he does:

FALSE RELIGIONS

2 Thessalonians 2:4-6 says, *"Who opposeth himself above all that is called God, or that is worshipped...* (This is when he destroys the whore Church, 3½ years into the Tribulation. He won't allow worship of any kind of religion, or any kind of god at all.) *...so that he as God sitteth in the temple of God, shewing himself that he is God. Remember ye not, that, when*

I was yet with you, I told you these things? And now ye know what, withholdeth (restrains him) *that he might be revealed in his time."*

Why do you know what withholds him? Because in Verse 3 Paul says, *"let no man deceive you, that day will not come until the departure of the Church takes place first."* That's why in this Verse he says, *"and now you know what withholds him."* Plain isn't it?

"And now ye know what withholds him that he may be revealed in his time." What is his time? It's the last week of Daniel's 70th week. A week the tuned-in Church won't be around for, because we will escape all of the Tribulation of that week.

2 Thessalonians 2:6,7, *"And now ye know what withholdeth that, he might be revealed in his time. For the mystery of iniquity doth already work:..."*

Jesus tells us through His Holy Spirit, through the apostle John, the spirit of Anti-Christ is at work, only there is a restraining force. What's the restraining force? The prayers of the saints, binding the devil. Our intercession in the Holy Ghost, casting out devils, preaching the Gospel, getting people born-again, preaching the good news.

2 Thessalonians 2:7, *"For the mystery of iniquity doth already work: only he who now letteth (or restrains will restrain) will let, until he be taken out of the way."*

Until he is taken out of the way. Now some people say that is the Holy Spirit. Well I'll tell you what, if the Holy Spirit goes, I go. My Bible tells me God will never leave me nor forsake me. So if the Holy Spirit goes, I go. But the Holy Spirit doesn't go, because people still get born-again during the Tribulation. The 144,000 witnesses preach the Gospel anointed of the

Holy Spirit. The Bible says they're sealed. What's the seal of God? It is the Holy Spirit. The two witnesses for the last 3½ years of the Tribulation, are anointed by God's Spirit. They witness and work signs through the power of the Holy Spirit.

The Church is the only person that is taken out of the way. What binds the devil? Jesus says, *"I will give you the keys of the kingdom. Whatever you bind on earth is bound, and whatever you loose is loosed, and the gates of hell won't prevail against My Church."*

> *"For the mystery of iniquity doth already work: only he who now letteth will let, until he be taken out of the way.*
>
> *And then shall that Wicked be revealed, whom the Lord shall consume with the spirit of his mouth, and shall destroy with the brightness of his coming:*
> *Even him, whose coming is after the working of Satan with all power and signs and lying wonders. And with all deceivableness of unrighteousness in them that perish; because they received not the love of the truth, that they might be saved"* (2 Thessalonians 2:7-10).

The unbeliever, not the born-again believer!

2 Thessalonians 2:11-17 says, *"And for this cause God shall send them strong delusion, that they should believe a lie: That they all might be damned who believed not the truth, but had pleasure in unrighteousness. But we are bound to give thanks always to God for you, brethren beloved of the Lord, because God hath from the beginning chosen you to salvation through sanctification of the Spirit and belief of the truth: Whereunto He called you by our gospel, to the obtaining of the glory of our Lord Jesus Christ.*

Therefore, brethren, stand fast, and hold the traditions which ye have been taught, whether by word, or our epistle.

Now our Lord Jesus Christ Himself, and God, even our Father, which hath loved us, and hath given us everlasting consolation and good hope through grace, Comfort your hearts, and establish you in every good word and work."

It's a very comforting thought to know that we go before he's revealed. Some people say that this is talking about backsliding. There is nothing comforting about backsliding. There is something very comforting about being taken away before the Anti-Christ is revealed and the Tribulation starts. Amen!

A possible rendering of this Verse, is the departure of the Church. It is possible, it is not incorrect in the Greek language, to render this Verse this way. And if you render the Verse this way, that's why Paul says, in Verse 6, *"And now you know."*

Why do you know? Because three verses before, he tells us, *"let no man deceive you by any means: for that day shall not come except there come a separation, except there come a departure of the Church, first, and the man of sin be revealed, the son of perdition;"*

> *"And now you know what withholdeth that he might be revealed in his time"* (2 Thessalonians 2:6).

And now you know what withholds him. It's you, the Church. *"...that he might be revealed in his time. ...for the spirit of the Anti-Christ is already at work, only he who restrains him will restrain him, until he is taken out of the way."* It's not angels, it is the Church of the Lord Jesus Christ, empowered by the Holy Spirit.

> *"And then shall that Wicked be revealed, whom the Lord shall consume with the spirit of his mouth, and shall destroy with the brightness of his coming"* (2 Thessalonians 2:8).

It is so simple when we study it in Chapter context, and don't pull isolated Verses out of the Bible, and try to make doctrines out of them.

Paul is not talking anywhere here about backsliding. He is talking about something being taken out of the way, so the Anti-Christ can be revealed.

The only vehicle which Jesus says the gates of hell won't prevail against, is His Church. Hallelujah! When we're taken out of the way, the Anti-Christ will be revealed in his time.

CHAPTER TWELVE

THE FOUR HORSES OF THE APOCALYPSE

I really believe that the days are close at hand when Jesus Christ is going to return.

I was interested to see on television recently a documentary on UFOs. Now the Pentagon has confirmed the existence of UFOs.

There's been sightings of UFOs again, and I recall saying many years ago that I believed that before Jesus returns there will be a resurrection of all these sightings of 'Unidentified Flying Objects', and that kind of phenomena.

As I looked at this program, I watched with amazement as they turned the UFOs into a doctrine for the New Age Movement.

The story said that a professor was supposedly taken up into this UFO and photographed it. The beings in the UFO communicated with crystals. Exactly what some New Agers use in their rituals.

They are Going to Have to Say Something to Explain the Rapture of the Church

The message these so called alien beings communicated by telepathy, to this professor was that he had to go and tell the world that they would soon contact mankind. Some people believe that in the very near future, these alien beings are going to contact mankind because mankind has 'evolved' (as soon as they start using evolution, we know it's from the kingdom of darkness; because we know we are not evolving, we know we were created) to a place now where they can start communicating with us. This will all be part of the deception to explain away the Rapture of the Church, when Christians disappear.

These beings say they are in 'harmony' with the 'supreme being of the universe.' They're not run by government but they're run by a federation. I thought, dear me, we know what we're soon heading to there will be a like-dictatorship, and a like-federation and coming together and uniting of nations. After the Church is taken out of the way at the Rapture, then this earth will be heading for One World Government.

The messages from these beings were that they were run by a federation and they don't have laws, they don't have any rules but they're all in love, and all at peace, and they're all in harmony, and they're all in unity one with another. All of these messages that these so-called alien beings gave this person to tell the world were just doctrines of the New Age Movement.

Sounds good, but all part of end-time deception. You can't have peace without Jesus because the heart of man is wicked and needs to be born again.

I thought OK, let's find out how true it is; let's listen to what these aliens are saying. No mention of Jesus, no mention of a Saviour and a Redeemer. Just that mankind is going to evolve into a higher being of consciousness. This is not possible without a relationship with Jesus Christ.

Mankind is not evolving. Civilization is degenerating from when God created us. God created us in a place of perfection and harmony, and we have degenerated from that place of perfection. We're not getting better; we're getting worse.

All over the world we are seeing lawlessness, as this spirit is at work. We are warned of this in the bible as a sign of the last days. It seems even rational people don't need much to suddenly go berserk – smashing windows, destroying lives and even killing people. On prime-time news we have seen groups of people, pull people out of their cars to bash them, during riots. The world has seemingly gone mad. This is a foretaste of just what it is going to be like in the Tribulation. Recent scenes and events in the country of Afghanistan have been very disturbing.

After the Rapture, the Anti-Christ will bring law and order through a total police state, and through the military.

> *"And I saw when the Lamb opened one of the seals, and I heard, as it were the noise of thunder, one of the four beasts saying, Come and see. And I saw, and behold a white horse: and he that sat on him had a bow; and a crown was given unto him: and he went forth conquering, and to conquer"* (Revelation 6:1,2).

He went forth conquering and to conquer! This is the Anti-Christ being revealed and released, after the church is taken out of the way.

God has already shown that the Lamb is Worthy, He is Worthy, to take the book from the Father, and to undo the seals, and in Verse 1 we see Jesus and He opens the first seal, and when He opens the first seal, the Angel says to John *'come and see.'*

Don't forget, John is standing before the throne, he is witnessing all of this. He is witnessing the Rapture of the Church, witnessing Jesus being crowned and receiving Glory from the Father, witnessing Jesus walk over to the Father and take the book that is sealed with seven seals, and witnessing Jesus open it up.

Then the Angel says to John, 'come and see what happens now in the earth', and he says *"...and I saw, and I behold a white horse:..."* Now this is the releasing of the Anti-Christ, after the Church is taken out of the earth. The Anti-Christ is let loose and he's let loose with the opening of the first seal.

The verse goes on, *"And I saw, and behold a white horse: and he that sat on him had a bow; and a crown was given unto him:..."* We know it is not Jesus. Jesus came and He defeated the devil in his own territory, and Jesus conquered, and He won His own crowns, hallelujah!

Jesus, the Bible says, has many crowns. He doesn't need a crown to be given to Him for a season so He can reign and rule on the earth. Jesus Christ is going to reign and rule for ever, and ever, because He is the King of Kings and the Lord of Lords. He has many crowns because He is King over many kings and that's us, hallelujah! We are redeemed unto our God by the blood of Jesus, that we should be Kings and Priests unto our God.

However, a crown is given unto the Anti-Christ and he goes forth conquering and to conquer. Jesus Christ doesn't have to do any more conquering – He's already conquered. He already has the keys of death and hell. He's already defeated Satan. He's already made a show of him openly, triumphing over him in it. His death on the cross. He triumphed over Satan and He rose from the dead as the conqueror and Supreme King.

The Anti-Christ goes forth for a season, conquering and to conquer, but the reason he is depicted here on a white horse is because he comes as a man of peace. But really he is a man of deception, only trying to imitate the real Christ.

That's why we are getting all this New Age, all this UFO nonsense – peace and harmony on the earth; we've all got to get in harmony with creation and with nature.

However, he can't bring peace because he has no peace. Satan will never be able to bring peace. The Anti-Christ will try to bring peace by using weapons of war and armies. Forcing people to comply to his will. Hence the scripture, he goes forth conquering and to conquer. It is an endeavour to bring the entire world under the control of Satan.

> *"And when he had opened the second seal, I heard the second beast say, Come and see. And there went*

out another horse that was red: and power was given to him that sat theron to take peace from the earth, and that they should kill one another: and there was given unto him a great sword" (Revelation 6:3,4).

Here we see the second horse and his rider and that's War. The rider on the red horse is War. A great sword is given to him (the great sword here is symbolic of War). There is only one way the Anti-Christ can subdue the earth, after the Church is taken out of the way, and that's by the force of War.

Lawlessness breaks forth, people begin breaking into buildings, stealing and killing, because suddenly the Church is gone. We were the restraining force of evil up until that point. Yes, because when we are taken out of the way all of the powers of darkness are released in this earth. The demons of Hell that have been thwarted in their activities for thousands of years because of the prayers of God's people; the spirits of darkness that have tried to rule and reign through mankind and bring out their expressions of hatred, murder and strife, and all of the other things of wickedness that have been suppressed by the prayers of God's people, because the gates of Hell cannot prevail against the Church.

When the Church is taken out of the way all these demons go berserk and a real spirit of lawlessness takes over the whole earth.

The only way the Anti-Christ can bring back law and order (understand that he wants to be world dictator, he wants the worship of mankind, he wants to run this place, the devil always wants to run this earth) is through War. Hence the rider on the red horse having the great sword. And so the second horse is let loose after the Church is taken out of the way.

> "And when he had opened the third seal, I heard the third beast say, Come and see. And I beheld, and lo a black horse; and he that sat on him had a pair of balances in his hand. And I heard a voice in the midst of the four beasts say, A measure of wheat for a penny, and three measures of barley for a penny; and see thou hurt not the oil and the wine" (Revelation 6:5,6).

This is Famine. Because famine always follows war. Because crops are going to be destroyed, the agricultural industry will be destroyed; and from people dying and being killed, there will be disease everywhere; not enough time to bury the bodies etc. There will be great famine, plagues and pestilences in the earth.

> "And when he had opened the fourth seal, I heard the voice of the fourth beast say, Come and see. And I looked, and behold a pale horse: and his name that sat on him was Death, and Hell followed with him. And power was given unto them over the fourth part of the earth, to kill with sword, and with hunger, and with death, and with the beasts of the earth" (Revelation 6:7,8).

Why? Why Death and Hell? Because as this so-called man of peace is let loose, the Anti-Christ, he is he, who comes after the working of Satan. Possessed by demonic power, eventually possessed by the devil himself. He brings a false peace to the earth, through war and weapons of war; a spirit of lawlessness prevails.

Pestilence and famine follow that War, and because of the famine, because of the disease and pestilences, then Great Death follows, and mankind starts to die. Then obviously Hell follows Death. Because without a Saviour, without Jesus, Hell is where the people are destined. They are destined to Hell without Jesus. And hence, Hell follows Death.

> *"...And power was given unto them over the fourth part of the earth, to kill with sword, and with hunger, and with death, and with the beasts of the earth"* (Revelation 6:8).

Why the beasts of the earth? When all this famine is taking place in the earth, the whole of the animal kingdom is going hungry, and starving; and the whole of the animal kingdom is also going to be taken over by this spirit of absolute lawlessness, and the animal kingdom is going to go into total revolt. Totally berserk. Imagine dogs in the Tribulation time, dogs that have been tied up and haven't been fed. There's no food, and they start to fight, to kill one another and to prey on human beings. That's what the Bible says – *"to kill with the beasts of the earth."* The animal kingdom is going to begin to prey on mankind!

Not nice days to be around! And some people tell us that God wants the Church to go through these things? God doesn't want the church to go through these things. God wants His people in heaven, praising Jesus, before this lawless one is revealed. He wants all His sons and daughters safe in His home in heaven, watching His Son receive Honour and Glory and Power as he takes the Book from the Father's hand and undoes the seals. He wants us worshipping and saying, 'Worthy are you, Oh Lord.'

That's why John sees the Church in heaven, praising Jesus. When he sees Jesus take the Book and open the first seal he goes over to the balconies of heaven and the angel says, *'Come and see what is happening in the earth.'* He sees these things and he has recorded it for us.

> *"For the Lord himself shall descend from heaven with a shout, with the voice of the archangel, and with the trump of God: and the dead in Christ shall rise first:"* (1 Thessalonians 4:16).

> *"For God hath not appointed us to wrath, but to obtain salvation by our Lord Jesus Christ, Who died for us, that, whether we wake or sleep, we should live together with him. Wherefore comfort yourselves together, and edify one another, even as also ye do"* (1 Thessalonians 5:9-11).

So the Church is not ignorant of what is to take place in the future on planet earth.

But only after the seven years of Tribulation and the Battle of Armageddon will the Prince of Peace, Jesus Christ, be able to usher in His one thousand year millennial reign of Peace. The Day of Christ.

CHAPTER THIRTEEN

JUDGEMENT AND MERCY

"And I went unto the angel, and said unto him, Give me the little book. And he said unto me, take it and eat it up; and it shall make thy belly bitter, but in thy mouth sweet as honey. And I took the little book out of the angel's hand, and ate it up; and it was in my mouth sweet as honey: and as soon as I had eaten it, my belly was bitter. And he said unto me, Thou must prophesy again before many peoples, and nations, and tongues, and kings" (Revelation 10:9-11).

Why is it as sweet as honey in his mouth? The Word of God brings Life. The Word of God is a Life Giving Word. The Word of God is a Delivering Word, and the Book of Revelation is a Book of comfort, and is a Book of peace, and it is a Book of joy. It is a comfort to those who know Jesus because we are going to miss out on those things. It encourages us to stay in with God, it encourages us to go on with God, and it says that there is a blessing for the person that hears, and reads, and does, the prophecy revealed in the Book of Revelation. In just reading this Book there is a blessing that is imparted to us, and as we become doers of this Word, we are blessed. There is a blessing on all the Word of God, but there is an extra blessing on the Book of Revelation.

Why is it bitter in the belly? Because God's Word is a two-edged sword. And the same Word that cuts for blessing, also cuts for judgement. God is a God of graciousness, and God is a long-suffering God. God is not willing that any should perish, but that all should come to repentance. At the moment we're under the grace of God, a time when we are to go into all the world and preach the Gospel unto every nation, and then the end shall come. There is coming a day in the not too distant future when the grace of God will come to an end, and the judgement of God will start to fall on planet earth. And for those who have not received and partaken of the grace of God and the blessings of God, the judgement of God is going to fall, and it is going to be bitter.

John had to go and preach this message, and for those who receive it, it would be as sweet as honey, but for those who reject it, it will be very bitter.

When we read these things in the Book of Revelation, they are horrific, they are terrible. The Bible says it is a fearful thing to fall into the hands of the living God.

God, for the last 2000 years has stretched forth His hand of mercy on this planet and He has said come unto Me and I will forgive you, for in Christ your sins are forgiven. Come unto Me and receive Sonship. Come unto Me and receive Kingship. Come unto Me and I will put a robe of righteousness on you. I will put a ring of Kingship on you. I will cause you to walk in a new way, with the Gospel of peace on your feet. You will be a fisher of men and spreader and sharer of the good news. I will make you a New Creation. I will make you My Son.

But the Bible also says, those that would not receive Jesus, the wrath of God abides upon them. There is coming a day, when Hell will follow Death. That's why it is bitter. Even though it is a fantastic Word, for those that receive Christ, God will also judge those that reject Him. This is the judgement side of God.

The Bible says, we are to have mercy on some, snatching them out of the fire. I really think that is a revelation that the Church has lost and needs to be restored. I know we can go overboard in a fire and brimstone message. However, hell is a real place and we can't sugarcoat, people who reject Christ go to hell. The coming judgement of God at the end of the Age of Grace, is a real and impending time that is to come. The message of how bad it will be during those last seven years of tribulation and for those that reject Christ, also needs to be preached.

Have you read Mary Baxter's book on her Revelation on Hell? I tell you what, it scares the Hell out of you when you do. I am warning you, you definitely do not want to go there.

The Word of God is a Life-giving Word. It is Life to you today. Today is the day of your Salvation. Don't reject Jesus. Don't walk away from God. Pray for your family, pray for this Nation. Pray for all people, because God is not willing that any should perish, but all be saved. There comes a day when He must judge this earth for its wickedness, in order to bring in everlasting peace; in order to bring in His goodness.

Some people, preachers and teachers, accuse God by saying he is going to leave His children here on this earth when these holocausts are poured out, and when the Anti-Christ is revealed.

God gave me the illustration of a sugarcane farmer up in North Queensland. "Shaun, does a sugarcane farmer, send his children out to play into the fields of cane when he is about to set light to them?" The answer to this question is of course, no!

A sugarcane farmer in Australia, sets light to the cane just before harvest, in order to prepare the cane for reaping. During this process all the toads, snakes, beetles and diseases are burned up. The farmer rids the fields of the dross and rubbish. No sugarcane farmer, in his right mind, would allow his children to play in those fields while they are burning. He would make sure His children are all safe in his home before the process begins! In the same manner, our Father God is going to bring His children home before He pours out His fiery judgement on this earth!

And yet there are those that accuse God, that when the judgement of God falls on this earth, that God is going to leave His children in the fields of the earth when He starts to burn the fields, and pour out His holocaust judgements on this earth.

No! God is not going to do that. God is going to take out His children. He is going to make sure His children are secure in His home before His end-time begins. While the church is here we are still in the age or dispensation of Grace

Sad to say, some of His family are going to resist that call. Some of God's family will be walking in rebellion to His Word, and they are going to have to get a bit scorched by fire. Even then there is a mid-tribulation Rapture of the Saints, if they repent. Some of them might have to lose their head or life by refusing to take the Mark, 666 as spoken of in Revelation 13: 16-18.

The Bible also reveals this, *"They that receive martyrdom, there is then a better resurrection, for they are rewarded for that, for resisting even unto death."* Hebrews 11:35. This is referring to not taking the mark of the beast (666) and or worshiping the Anti-Christ and following his doctrines.

Don't you be of those that rebel and miss out on the Rapture. Repent today and put your life right with God and walk according to the Word and not according to the flesh. WATCH and pray so you are Raptured Ready, when on that great day when the Father sends his Son to bring the family home to Him.

> *"For the Lord himself shall descend from heaven with a shout, with the voice of the archangel, and with the trump of God: and the dead in Christ shall rise first: Then we which are alive and remain shall be caught up together with them in the clouds, to meet the Lord in the air: and so shall we ever be with the*

Lord. Wherefore comfort one another with these words" (1 Thessalonians 4:16-18).

Chapter Fourteen

MY DREAM

God gave me a dream some time back, and I want to share it with you.

> *"And they shall fall by the edge of the sword, and shall be led away captive into all nations: ...* (talking about the Nation of Israel, the Jews) *... and Jerusalem shall be trodden down of the Gentiles, until the times of the Gentiles be fulfilled"* (Luke 21:24).

The time of the Gentiles is fulfilled at the Rapture of the Church, when God starts dealing again with the Nation of Israel in a very real and powerful way. The last 2000 years have been the Gentile Nations preaching the Gospel. The Bible says Jerusalem will be trodden down of the Gentiles. We know that Israel became a Nation in 1948, we know that they retook the old city Jerusalem in 1967, Jesus states that those that witness this will be the last generation.

According to Psalm 90:10 a generation is somewhere between seventy to eighty years.

> "The days of our lives are seventy years; and if by reason of strength they are eighty years, yet their boast is only labour and sorrow; For it is soon cut off, and we fly away" (Psalm 90:10).

> "And He spoke to them a parable; Behold the fig tree, and all the trees; When they now shoot forth, ye see and know of your own selves that summer is now nigh at hand. So likewise you, when you see these things come to pass, know ye that the kingdom of God is near at hand. Truly I say unto you, this generation shall not pass away, till all be fulfilled" (Luke 21:29-32).

When you see what things come to pass?
1. The Jews coming back home from captivity. We have seen and are seeing this come to pass.
2. Israel has become a Nation again. Israel, as a nation didn't exist for 2000 years, but in 1948 Israel was born again; people that are living today have seen this prophecy fulfilled.
3. Jerusalem was recaptured in 1967 and recognised by the nations of the world, as the capital of Israel again in 2017.

Jerusalem recognised as the capital of Israel in 2017 coincided with the 120th Jubilee year.

He says, *"likewise when you see these things come to pass, know you that the Kingdom of God is at hand."* And He says, *"Truly I say unto you, this generation..."* Which generation? The generation that sees these things come to pass, it shall not all pass away till all things be fulfilled. And Jesus says, *"Heaven and earth shall pass away: but my words..."* these words He has just spoken... *"shall not pass away."*

Jesus says, *"this Word will not pass away, until the things He has just spoken about are all fulfilled. The generation that sees these things come to pass will not all pass away, till all things be fulfilled."*

We are without a doubt the last generation!

> *"And there shall be signs in the sun, and in the moon, and in the stars; and upon the earth distress of nations... (that is what we are seeing right now, the distress of nations) ...with perplexity; the sea and the waves roaring; Men's hearts failing them for fear, and for looking after those things which are coming on the earth: for the powers of heaven shall be shaken"* (Luke 21:25,26).

In the above scripture Jesus mentions great fear coming into peoples' hearts in the last days. Take the Corona pandemic for instance. This pandemic has caused so much fear, stress and heartache to every nation on earth! The world has never seen the likes of this before! Practically no nation was spared it's reach and the problems it has caused.

The ongoing repercussion of this virus/plague is still yet to be known. Lives have been lost, businesses destroyed, and everyday life and the way we go about it has been disrupted worldwide. Fear caused by this and other tragic events, such as the wildfires we have seen in Australia, Europe and America, are causing huge loss of life, flora and fauna and financial devastation. The world is witnessing a dramatic increase in earthquake activity. As Jesus foretold in the Gospels, it is literally happening in every quarter of the earth at the same time. We could also speak about famines caused by droughts, locust plagues of biblical proportions have been reported all over the world by the media. At the same time, some countries are experiencing terrible droughts. Other countries are experiencing unusual floods, mudslides that are destroying whole towns and villages. We could go on and talk about tsunamis, cyclones and devastating storms. These and other natural events are all on the increase.

Jesus also said that the powers of heaven would be shaken. There is unusual activity and solar flares that have been recorded in our sun. Asteroids like Apophis are hurtling towards the earth at astronomical speeds. If one such asteroid was to hit the earth, it would have cataclysmic consequences. In the book of Revelation, it speaks of these events.

The asteroid Apophis will come closer to the earth than more than 500 of our geostationary satellites that are in orbit. In astronomical terms, this is a hair's breath from our planet. Ten times closer than the moon. It will be the closest asteroid of its size in recorded history. This event is to take place on Friday, April 13th 2029.

There are over 19,000 near Earth objects (NEOs) that NASA has discovered and is tracking. They are discovering an average of 30 new ones a week. This represents an increase of 50% since 2013. NASA is working on a new plan to detect and destroy asteroids before they hit the earth. Jesus prophesied that in the last days stars would fall from heaven to the earth like a fig tree shaking its figs.

According to the words of Jesus, we are in the last days!

We are going to see some funny things happen in the heavens, and they can tell us it is UFOs even the Pentagon now confirms the existence of UFOs. Yet they have no explanation for them. The Bible says, "Men's hearts failing them for fear..." God gives you a dream and after you study His Word, that confirms the dream.

> *"Men's hearts failing them for fear, and for looking after those things which are coming on the earth: for the powers of heaven shall be shaken"* (Luke 21:26).

God gave me a dream some time back and I want to share it with you.

And so I had this dream and I thank God He gave me the first part of the dream first; because this dream was so real I thought it was happening.

I had gone to bed, and then suddenly found I had been Raptured, and here I was, standing in the reception room of heaven. (I am not saying this is how it is. God shows us things we can understand with our mind.) Here I was, booking in. You know what it is like when you stay in a Hotel, you go up to the reception where all the people are working behind the desk and they get out the book and check you in, then the porter comes and takes your bags for you.

So here I was, standing in the Reception Rooms of Heaven and I thought, 'wow I have been Raptured.' The angels were there and they were really, really busy and they were bringing out these books, and I was thinking, 'I hope my name's in this book here.' There were people all around me, and all hustle and bustle. Loads and loads of people that had been Raptured, all at the check-in counters of Heaven, and the angels going through the books and ticking off their names. And nearby there were racks and racks and racks of these big white garments, and the angels were going through them and calling names and matching the robes. A person would take his robe and go over to the changing room and put on his 'new robe.' When you had put on your robe you had to go through this door.

And I just knew, that I knew, that I knew, that on the other side of that door was the Lord Jesus Christ.

Every fibre of my being wanted to go through that door, and meet my Saviour. Every fibre of my being! The angels were going through the books and I was thinking, 'I hope my name's there, I hope I did not get picked up just by accident.' It was just such an awesome feeling. The whole air was just permeated with holiness and reverence and a purity for Almighty God. Every fibre of my being wanted to go through that door, then suddenly I thought, 'I do not want to go through that door.' It was like a fear and I didn't want to go through that door. I didn't feel worthy.

Here I am, I did not know that this day was going to take place so quickly. Then all of a sudden here I am, raptured and in heaven. I was aware of my thoughts, they were coming to me rapidly, things like, "There are things I have not done, things I have not attended to. And now I have to go and meet Jesus. I will have to give an account of everything I have ever done." It was just like my whole life was exposed. I could not hide anything. I am going to meet Jesus. Every bit of me wanted to go through the door, but then I did not want to go through.

I was fighting this kind of fight in me, and as I was wrestling with it, suddenly this great peace came over me, and I knew, 'but by His blood I'm worthy to go through that door.' No man's worthy in himself, and we have all got things we have not attended to, and we have all got things we have not done, and I thought 'but by His blood', and a great peace swept over my being, and I was ready then to go through the door. I was ready to rush into the arms of Jesus, and the dream ended.

I never did get to see Jesus, never did get to go through the door, but what God was showing me, in that part of the dream was how it is not by works of the law that we are saved but through the blood of Jesus Christ.

And what God also showed me was, that on that day, our minds are just so expanded, that we are just so aware of what we have done, and also what we have not done. And I thought, 'Oh there are people I have not witnessed to, there are people that God told me to witness to, and I have not witnessed to them.'

I went through all these emotions, and I realised it was His love, and His grace that would be sufficient for me to go through that door. I snapped out of that dream and I thought I have really got to go and get more on fire for God. Get more zealous for the things of God. I am going to preach better sermons, preach longer sermons, and whatever He wants me to do I'm just going to do it.

I'm just going to be faithful because He wants us to be faithful. We are never going to be perfect this side of Heaven, but God wants us to be faithful. We will make mistakes but God doesn't want us to live in our mistakes and walk in rebellion to Him. If we make a mistake be quick to repent. If someone sins against us, be quick to forgive them, and be quick to get up and get going again serving God. Stay in that secret place of intimacy with the Lord. Do not hold things against your brothers, sisters, friends of family for 10 years, 5 years, or even a year. Not even a day for that matter! Do not hold things against your wives or your husbands. Don't let the sun go down on our wrath because tonight Jesus might come!

Put things right, stay in that place. Walk in that place of forgiveness. Walk in that place of being quick to forgive, quick to repent, quick to get about our Father's business again.

I went straight into the second part of the dream. This time I had missed the Rapture. I tell you I am glad that the other dream came first, or I reckon if I had the second part first I would have freaked out. But I knew I was OK, and God was only putting me through experiences.

This time, I woke up, and I knew I had missed out on the Rapture. My wife was beside me; I hadn't seen a newspaper, or hadn't heard a television report, hadn't heard a radio report, but when I woke up I knew that the Rapture had taken place.

It was like the air, instead of being permeated with peace and holiness, it was permeated with fear. And then God showed me this Scripture, "men's hearts failing them for fear."

Some people think, 'Oh well too bad if I miss out on the Rapture, I will just repent and it will be OK', but what God showed me in this dream, the one thing that really hit me, was that if you can't live for God this side of the Rapture, it is going to be very, very hard to live for God on the other side.

It is going to be death for those that refuse to worship the beast and take his number, 666. Satan and his army are going to torment people. He is going to force people that do not want that mark, in some way which will be revealed at that time. You will not be able to buy, sell or do business in any description without that mark and number. It is a system of forced worship, submission, total domination and control of your life.

In the middle of those last seven years, the Anti-Christ will proclaim himself God and backed by the False Prophet, he will force people to start receiving the mark. It is a system that will control the entire commerce of the earth.

If you think it requires too much of your life to serve God now, then on the other side of the Rapture it really is, literally, going to require peoples' lives. Satan is going to put people to death who do not take his mark, the number of the beast. He is going to kill them, and torture them to receive that mark of the beast.

The Scripture says, **"men's hearts failing them for fear."**

I woke up and there was my wife, and the air was literally permeated with fear. Unbelievable to describe. The only thought that I had was to wake my wife, do not worry about the house, do not worry about packing our bags or anything; grab a few things and run. Get in our car and drive. We raced out, got in the car and started to drive, all I could think of was, get out of the city. Get away from every single person and collect my thoughts somewhere else.

Because I had great fear, I just knew there would be rank lawlessness and people would go berserk. And that is just what happened. Here I was driving down the road, my wife beside me, and people were just rushing out of their houses, people were breaking into houses.

It was as though sometime during the night the Rapture had taken place and people just knew something had happened and they had gone out of their minds. People were already running up and down pillaging houses, people in the middle of the street, people waving, 'stop, stop, stop.' I had one thought, 'do not stop, just put your foot down on the accelerator and speed around them to get out of town. Get out in the country somewhere, where there is no people.'

And then the dream ended and I woke up and thought, I'm glad I'm awake.

The main thing that God impressed on me was the spirit of fear that literally permeates the earth when the Church is taken out of the way.

There is no explaining this feeling.

It is the Church that binds the spirit of fear. It is the Church that brings peace. Jesus says, *"Peace I leave you with: My peace I give unto you."* We have the peace of God, and the Bible says the Church is the light of the earth, and the Church is the salt of the earth. I tell you, when the salt is taken out of the earth, (salt is a preservative; that is what they used it for in olden times; without salt meat went bad), this earth goes bad.

The bible says the Church is the light of the world, and when the light is taken out of the earth, darkness reigns and rules in this earth.

It will be like the whole earth, overnight, will be permeated with fear. The whole atmosphere will be charged with fear. People everywhere will be going out of their minds.

Fear activates the curse and darkness in the same way faith activates the blessing.

I believe, after that, the Anti-Christ is revealed, and he goes forth conquering and to conquer. At first, he comes as a man of peace. Why? He comes to restore peace to this earth. Peace that has left after the Church has been caught away.

And so people then start to turn their allegiance to him, the Anti-Christ. He will be like their Saviour, their deliverer, as he starts to bring law and order back to the lawlessness. But he is the ruler of lawlessness himself, and so he will be a law unto himself.

And that is what God showed me in my dream.

So thank God the Church is the light of the earth. Thank God the Church is the salt of the earth. And thank God that we are here to bind and break the enemy's power; we are here to preserve this planet. We are here to show the light of the Gospel in this place so that men can be saved, until the great catching up or Rapture!

Remember the Church, that's you and me, and our brothers and sisters in the Body of Christ, are the salt of the earth. Salt was a preservative in the ancient world to preserve meat and when there was not salt the meat went rotten, so when the salt (the Church) is removed from the earth, it will go terribly rotten. The Church is here to be the preservative of the world. **The salt of the earth.**

Chapter Fifteen

THE RAPTURE, AS REVEALED IN THE ANCIENT JEWISH WEDDING

I have been a student of the biblical teaching on eschatology and the Rapture of the Church for many years. Over this time I have taught countless messages and sermons on it. After one such message a visitor to my church asked me the question, "Have you seen the Rapture in the Ancient Jewish Wedding?" Well that immediately got my attention. He said, "There are many references in the bible to marriage when it comes to God and His people."

Immediately scriptures started going off on the inside of me! I went home and commenced my study on the Ancient Jewish Wedding. Here I present, in this chapter, some of the things I discovered and a greater appreciation of the love that Jesus Christ has for His church. It is likened to the love of a young couple, newly engaged leading to the marriage of that couple.

I have found a whole new appreciation for the Song of Solomon and the love between the Bridegroom and His betrothed, the love of His life!

As I read the Song of Solomon again, God spoke to me about the verse in chapter one, verse two.

"Let him kiss me with the kisses of his mouth—for your love is better than wine" (Song of Solomon 1:2).

A Revelation is a Kiss From God

The Lord said to me, "Shaun, a revelation is a kiss from God", "When I kiss you, I am giving you revelations, to empower you to win in life through Jesus Christ!"

A study of the word 'kiss' here, is the Hebrew word 'Nashaq'. This word means to equip or arm for battle! We need God's kisses, God's revelation knowledge, revealed to us by the Holy Spirit, through Jesus Christ to become His equipped warriors. Remember, you are called to reign and rule in life, through Jesus Christ. (Romans 5:17).

One piece of literature I read while doing my study, was a book titled *'The Ancient Jewish Wedding'* by Jamie Lash.

It is a well written and well researched piece of work on the Ancient Jewish Wedding and has been a valuable tool and point of reference study for some of the thoughts I have presented in this chapter. In the footnotes, I have included details of where you can find this book, if you want to research this yourself further. I have expanded and added to this wonderful truth, as I have seen for myself the rapture in the Ancient Jewish ceremony as referred to by Jesus in His parables. After seeking the Lord and much prayer, I felt that this work would not be complete if I didn't add this revelation.

I have prayed and asked the Lord to help me reveal the deep and hidden truths that I have seen confirmed in the Word. I have asked Him to give me the ability to present them to you in this chapter in a concise and easy way for you to understand. I pray that you are greatly blessed, encouraged, empowered and comforted, as you read this exciting chapter.

> *"Then shall the kingdom of heaven be likened unto ten virgins, which took their lamps, and went forth to meet the bridegroom. And five of them were wise, and five were foolish. They that were foolish took their lamps, and took no oil with them: But the wise took oil in their vessels with their lamps. While the bridegroom tarried, they all slumbered and slept. And at midnight there was a cry made, Behold, the bridegroom cometh; go ye out to meet him. Then all those virgins arose, and trimmed their lamps. And the foolish said unto the wise, Give us of your oil; for our lamps are gone out. But the wise answered, saying, Not so; lest there be not enough for us and you: but go ye rather to them that sell, and buy for yourselves. And while they went to buy, the bridegroom came; and they that were ready went in with him to the marriage: and the door was shut. Afterward came also the other virgins, saying, Lord, Lord, open to us. But he answered and said, Verily I say unto you, I know you not. Watch therefore, for ye know neither the day nor the hour wherein the Son of man cometh"* (Matthew 25: 1-13).

In the above scripture, we can see how Jesus refers to Himself as the Bridegroom. We are going to look at God's great love relationship for His people and see The Rapture or 'Catching Up' of the church, as depicted in the Ancient Jewish Wedding. One other thing that I would also like to point out from the above scripture, is the fact that only half the virgins were ready when the Bridegroom came. The ones with no oil in their lamps asked the ones with oil, for some of their oil. To which this group replied, *"No, in case there is not enough for us."* Here we see the importance of every Believer having their own personal relationship with Jesus and keeping their lamps or light burning, by feeding on the Word and being led by the Spirit of God.

The bible chronicles the love relationship between God and His people. This is revealed strongly in the book 'Song of Solomon'. In the Word, we see the marriage of God to Israel and the marriage covenant that He kept and honoured, even though His people didn't.

It also reveals in the New Testament, God's new covenant for both Jews and non-Jews. We must understand the fullness of the word 'marriage'. It means, "the relationship that exists between two people who are united as spouses: the state of being married." In addition to this, marriage also means; a close union of or between two or more things; a marriage of sweet and spicy flavours; a marriage of science and art; a marriage between form and function; a marriage of jazz, blues, and pop.

I see three marriages in the bible. The first one is between God and Israel, this is the old covenant. The second is between both the Jews and the Gentiles, through the born-again experience and receiving Jesus Christ as Lord. Please read the following verses to see the first two covenants or marriages.

> *"Behold, the days are coming, says the Lord, when I will make a new covenant with the house of Israel and with the house of Judah— not according to the covenant that I made with their fathers in the day that I took them by the hand to lead them out of the land of Egypt, My covenant which they broke, though I was a husband to them, says the Lord. But this is the covenant that I will make with the house of Israel after those days, says the Lord: I will put My law in their minds, and write it on their hearts; and I will be their God, and they shall be My people. No more shall every man teach his neighbour, and every man his brother, saying, 'Know the Lord,' for they all shall know Me, from the least of them to the greatest of them, says the Lord. For I will forgive their iniquity, and their sin I will remember no more"* (Jeremiah 31:31-34).

The third marriage will be at the end of the millennial reign, after the great white throne judgement. It will be a culmination of all things, and the beginnings of the new heaven and earth. The New Jerusalem will then descend like a bride out of heaven to the new earth. God the Father will be present physically in the midst of this and Jesus Christ will march triumphantly into this New Jerusalem. He will then present to the Father all His sons and daughters, from all generations and dispensations, who have been redeemed by the blood and follow the Lamb. This will be the last great marriage of all things together and we will then go on into the eternal Kingdom to come, in the presence of the Father, the Son and the Holy Spirit.

It will be the greatest day of rejoicing ever, and this day will never cease, not for all eternity.

> "For Zion's sake I will not hold My peace, and for Jerusalem's sake I will not rest, until her righteousness goes forth as brightness, and her salvation as a lamp that burns. The Gentiles shall see your righteousness, and all kings your glory. You shall be called by a new name, which the mouth of the Lord will name. You shall also be a crown of glory in the hand of the Lord, and a royal diadem in the hand of your God. You shall no longer be termed Forsaken, nor shall your land any more be termed Desolate; But you shall be called Hephzibah, and your land Beulah; for the Lord delights in you, and your land shall be married. For as a young man marries a virgin, so shall your sons marry you; And as the bridegroom rejoices over the bride, so shall your God rejoice over you. I have set watchmen on your walls, O Jerusalem; they shall never hold their peace day or night. You who make mention of the Lord, do not keep silent, and give Him no rest till He establishes and till He makes Jerusalem a praise in the earth. The Lord has sworn by His right hand and by the arm of His strength:

"Surely I will no longer give your grain as food for your enemies; And the sons of the foreigner shall not drink your new wine, for which you have labored. But those who have gathered it shall eat it, and praise the Lord; Those who have brought it together shall drink it in My holy courts." Go through, go through the gates! Prepare the way for the people; build up, build up the highway! Take out the stones, lift up a banner for the peoples! Indeed the Lord has proclaimed to the end of the world: "Say to the daughter of Zion, 'Surely your salvation is coming; Behold, His reward is with Him, and His work before Him.' "And they shall call them The Holy People, the Redeemed of the Lord; And you shall be called Sought Out, a City Not Forsaken" (Isaiah 62: 1-12 NKJV).

"Now I saw a new heaven and a new earth, for the first heaven and the first earth had passed away. Also there was no more sea. Then I, John, saw the holy city, New Jerusalem, coming down out of heaven from God, prepared as a bride adorned for her husband. And I heard a loud voice from heaven saying, "Behold, the tabernacle of God is with men, and He will dwell with them, and they shall be His people. God Himself will be with them and be their God. And God will wipe away every tear from their eyes; there shall be no more death, nor sorrow, nor crying. There shall be no more pain, for the former things have passed away."

Then He who sat on the throne said, "Behold, I make all things new." And He said to me, "Write, for these words are true and faithful." And He said to me, "It is done! I am the Alpha and the Omega, the Beginning and the End. I will give of the fountain of the water of life freely to him who thirsts. He who overcomes shall inherit all things, and I will be his God and he shall be My son. But the cowardly, unbelieving, abominable, murderers, sexually immoral, sorcerers, idolaters, and all liars shall have their part in the lake which burns with fire and brimstone, which is the second death." Then one of the seven angels who had the seven bowls filled with the seven last plagues came to me and talked with me, saying, "Come, I will show you the bride, the Lamb's wife." And he carried me away in the Spirit to a great and high mountain, and showed me the great city, the holy Jerusalem, descending out of heaven from God, having the glory of God. Her light was like a most precious stone, like a jasper stone, clear as crystal. Also she had a great and high wall with twelve gates, and twelve angels at the gates, and names written on them, which are the names of the twelve tribes of the children of Israel: three gates on the east, three gates on the north, three gates on the south, and three gates on the west. Now the wall of the city had twelve foundations, and on them were the names of the twelve apostles of the Lamb" (Revelation 21:1-14 NKJV).

When the sixth dispensation, which was the dispensation of law or Old Covenant was fulfilled, the seventh dispensation of the Church Age or Age of Grace began. This was the New Covenant. This dispensation will end at The Rapture. After the eighth dispensation of time, this is the millennial reign of Christ that lasts for one thousand years. The last and final dispensation will begin which is the dispensation of the eternal Kingdoms to come and a never ending time of God's physical presence, goodness and glory.

> *"But I saw no temple in it, for the Lord God Almighty and the Lamb are it's temple. The city had no need of the sun or of the moon to shine in it, for the glory of God illuminated it. The Lamb is it's light. And the nations of those who are saved shall walk in it's light, and the kings of the earth bring their glory and honor into it. It's gates shall not be shut at all by day (there shall be no night there). And they shall bring the glory and the honor of the nations into it. But there shall by no means enter it anything that defiles, or causes an abomination or a lie, but only those who are written in the Lamb's Book of Life"* (Revelation 21:22-27).

> *"That in the ages to come He might show the exceeding riches of His grace in His kindness toward us in Christ Jesus"* (Ephesians 2:7).

The Now Let's Look at Our Marriage to Jesus

> *"But some of these branches from Abraham's tree—some of the people of Israel—have been broken off. And you Gentiles, who were branches from a wild olive tree, have been grafted in. So now you also receive the blessing God has promised Abraham and his children, sharing in the rich nourishment from the root of God's special olive tree"* (Romans 11:17 NLT).

Through the power of the Holy Spirit and our acceptance of Jesus Christ as Lord and Saviour, we have been grafted in, born into, baptized into that one body. We have become one with God, through our Lord Jesus Christ. This is a marriage. We are joined as one together with the Lord.

> *"As the Scriptures say, "A man leaves his father and mother and is joined to his wife, and the two are united into one." This is a great mystery, but it is an illustration of the way Christ and the church are one"* (Ephesians 5:31-32 NLT).
>
> *"I am overwhelmed with joy in the Lord my God! For he has dressed me with the clothing of salvation and draped me in a robe of righteousness. I am like a bridegroom dressed for his wedding or a bride with her jewels"* (Isaiah 61:10 NLT).

As you can see, there is a lot of marriage talk and revelation concerning a relationship with God and the Lord Jesus Christ. We are to adorn ourselves with jewels. I believe this is a reference to growing in the Word of God. We are growing in the Christian faith, adding to our faith the character and gifts of the Holy Spirit, developing the fruit of the Spirit and flowing in His gifts.

> *"But the fruit of the Spirit is love, joy, peace, longsuffering, kindness, goodness, faithfulness, gentleness, self-control. Against such there is no law. And those who are Christ's have crucified the flesh with its passions and desires. If we live in the Spirit, let us also walk in the Spirit"* (Galatians 5:22-25 NKJV).

> *"And be not drunk with wine, wherein is excess; but be filled with the Spirit"* (Ephesians 5:18).

How to Keep Your Lamp Filled

"Simon Peter, a bondservant and apostle of Jesus Christ, to those who have obtained like precious faith with us by the righteousness of our God and Savior Jesus Christ: Grace and peace be multiplied to you in the knowledge of God and of Jesus our Lord, as His divine power has given to us all things that pertain to life and godliness, through the knowledge of Him who called us by glory and virtue, by which have been given to us exceedingly great and precious promises, that through these you may be partakers of the divine nature, having escaped the corruption that is in the world through lust. But also for this very reason, giving all diligence, add to your faith

virtue, to virtue knowledge, to knowledge self-control, to self-control perseverance, to perseverance godliness, to godliness brotherly kindness, and to brotherly kindness love. For if these things are yours and abound, you will be neither barren nor unfruitful in the knowledge of our Lord Jesus Christ. For he who lacks these things is short-sighted, even to blindness, and has forgotten that he was cleansed from his old sins. Therefore, brethren, be even more diligent to make your call and election sure, for if you do these things you will never stumble; for so an entrance will be supplied to you abundantly into the everlasting kingdom of our Lord and Savior Jesus Christ. For this reason I will not be negligent to remind you always of these things, though you know and are established in the present truth" (2 Peter 1:1-12 NKJV).

Our Relationship with Jesus is Likened to that of a Bride

"For I am jealous for you with godly jealousy. For I have betrothed you to one husband, that I may present you as a chaste virgin to Christ. But I fear, lest somehow, as the serpent deceived Eve by his craftiness, so your minds may be corrupted from the simplicity that is in Christ" (2 Corinthians 11:2-3).

Here we can see in the above scripture that the Apostle Paul desires to present us, the Believers, individually and collectively as a chaste virgin to Christ. He is concerned that the devil may try to corrupt our minds away from the simplicity that is in Christ and His Word. Paul put everything on the line; his reputation, his finances, his social status, his own mind and his own body. He did this in order to serve God by serving the Church and laying down His life for it, even as Jesus did for us. Paul gave his all, that the power of Christ would rest upon him, so that he could walk in promises, signs, wonders and mighty deeds. We have the great revelations that build us up in the faith, and make us strong in the spirit that Christ delivered to the Apostle Paul.

In 2 Corinthians 11:2, we see the word 'betrothed', which means engaged. Even though we are born-again and one with Jesus, all Believers are in some way, both male and female, spiritually engaged to a Bridegroom. We are not physically present with the Lord. He is in the third heaven, His Father's house, preparing a place for us. He will come and take us to that place at The Rapture.

> "Therefore, my brethren, you also have become dead to the law through the body of Christ, that you may be married to another—to Him who was raised from the dead, that we should bear fruit to God" (Romans 7:4 NKJV).

Here we see in this scripture, we have died to the law, which was the first marriage contract. We are now married to Jesus Christ, we have become one with Him, part of His body by the power of the Holy Spirit. We now have a new marriage contract or covenant.

A person is bound by their first marriage (unless there is divorce) until the person dies. They are then free to marry again. A second marriage occurs with a new covenant or contract. I like to say out of intimacy comes great fruitfulness. The purpose of our union to God now, is to bear fruit, fruit resulting in the salvation of souls.

> *"The fruit of the righteous is a tree of life; and he that wins souls is wise"* (Proverbs 11:30).

The most intimate relationship that can exist between two human beings is the marriage relationship. God created this relationship between Adam and Eve in the Garden of Eden. He told them to go forth, increase and multiply and have dominion on the earth. In the same way, we now become one with our Lord Jesus Christ, through the born-again experience.

> *"For this cause shall a man leave his father and mother, and shall be joined unto his wife, and they two shall be one flesh. This is a great mystery: but I speak concerning Christ and the church" (Ephesians 5:31-32).*

This is a picture of our relationship with Jesus and the intimacy that every individual believer can have with God. We are captured by His love, cleansed by His blood and transformed by His Spirit. We bear fruit for Him until the day we stand before Him, without spot or wrinkle, at the Rapture or catching up of the church. As the Bridegroom says in the Song of Solomon 4:7, *"You are all fair, my love, and there is no spot in you."*

Jesus is the One who accomplishes this work in us by His Spirit. From faith to faith and from glory to glory!

Selection of the Bride

In Ancient Israel, brides were usually chosen by the Father of the Bridegroom. He would send his most trusted servant to search for a bride for his son. We see in the book of Genesis, an example of this.

> *"So Abraham said to the oldest servant of his house, who ruled over all that he had, "Please, put your hand under my thigh, and I will make you swear by the Lord, the God of heaven and the God of the earth, that you will not take a wife for my son from the daughters of the Canaanites, among whom I dwell; but you shall go to my country and to my family, and take a wife for my son Isaac." And the servant said to him, "Perhaps the woman will not be willing to follow me to this land. Must I take your son back to the land from which you came?" But Abraham said to him, "Beware that you do not take my son back there. The Lord God of heaven, who took me from my father's house and from the land of my family, and who spoke to me and swore to me, saying, 'To your descendants I give this land,' He will send His angel before you, and you shall take a wife for my son from there. And if the woman is not willing to follow you, then you will be released from this oath; only do not take my*

> *son back there." So the servant put his hand under the thigh of Abraham his master, and swore to him concerning this matter"* (Genesis 24:2-9 NKJV).

So Abraham sent his most trusted servant Eleizer, whose name means "God's helper". He was a type of the Holy Spirit. So Abraham chose, in this sense, Isaac's wife. The Father of the Bridegroom would always act in the best interest of his son, in choosing his bride. In the new covenant or testament we see a spiritual application of this old covenant custom.

> *"You did not choose Me, but I chose you and appointed you that you should go and bear fruit, and that your fruit should remain, that whatever you ask the Father in My name He may give you"* (John 15:16 NKJV).

Here we can see that we were chosen by God. Both the natural Jew and also the Gentile (you and me) have been chosen by the Father to be one with Christ. It is the Holy Spirit who convicts us and draws us unto God, through the Lord Jesus Christ. We have a choice to accept or reject this work of grace. We are, both Jew and Gentile, all recipients of the same love and accepted in the beloved.

> *"To the praise of the glory of His grace, by which He made us accepted in the Beloved"* (Ephesians 1:6 NKJV).

We love our Bridegroom and enjoy fellowshipping with Him in His Word, through the power of the Holy Spirit.

> *"Whom having not seen you love. Though now you do not see Him, yet believing, you rejoice with joy inexpressible and full of glory"* (1 Peter 1:8 NKJV).

We do not yet see Jesus, with our physical eye, yet we love and believe in Him. On the day of The Rapture, or the catching up of the church we will see Him face to face.

Another example of a Father obtaining a wife for his son in the old covenant was that of Samson.

> *"Now Samson went down to Timnah, and saw a woman in Timnah of the daughters of the Philistines. So he went up and told his father and mother, saying, "I have seen a woman in Timnah of the daughters of the Philistines; now therefore, get her for me as a wife." Then his father and mother said to him, "Is there no woman among the daughters of your brethren, or among all my people, that you must go and get a wife from the uncircumcised Philistines? And Samson said to his father, "Get her for me, for she pleases me well"* (Judges 14:1-3 NKJV),

We will expand this a little bit more, further in this chapter.

> *"And Jesus answered and spoke to them again by parables and said: "The kingdom of heaven is like a certain king who arranged a marriage for his son, and sent out his servants to call those who were*

invited to the wedding; and they were not willing to come. Again, he sent out other servants, saying, 'Tell those who are invited, "See, I have prepared my dinner; my oxen and fatted cattle are killed, and all things are ready. Come to the wedding."' But they made light of it and went their ways, one to his own farm, another to his business. And the rest seized his servants, treated them spitefully, and killed them. But when the king heard about it, he was furious. And he sent out his armies, destroyed those murderers, and burned up their city. Then he said to his servants, 'The wedding is ready, but those who were invited were not worthy. Therefore go into the highways, and as many as you find, invite to the wedding.' So those servants went out into the highways and gathered together all whom they found, both bad and good. And the wedding hall was filled with guests. "But when the king came in to see the guests, he saw a man there who did not have on a wedding garment. So he said to him, 'Friend, how did you come in here without a wedding garment?' And he was speechless. Then the king said to the servants, 'Bind him hand and foot, take him away, and cast him into outer darkness; there will be weeping and gnashing of teeth.' "For many are called, but few are chosen" (Matthew 22:1-20 NKJV).

The Love Relationship

Jesus as a Jewish Bridegroom always initiates the love. We didn't select Him, He selected us. 1 John 4:19 tells us, *"We love Him because He first loved us."*

He loves us because He has chosen us, and He has chosen us because He loves us.

"When a man takes a wife" (Deuteronomy 24:1a).

The Hebrew word or term 'takes' used here is 'laqach'. This is also a business term, meaning a transaction has taken place. i.e. *"Takes, especially buy, be taken in marriage, to be lifted up and take or carried away."*

When a man took or acquired a wife in Ancient Israel, there was a dowry paid to the Father of the Bride, both to compensate him for the loss of a worker in his household and also to demonstrate the great value that the Bridegroom placed upon the Bride. Remember the price that God paid to purchase or redeem us!

"Therefore take heed to yourselves and to all the flock, among which the Holy Spirit has made you overseers, to shepherd the church of God which He purchased with His own blood" (Acts 20:28 NKJV).

Selah, pause and think about this for a moment. We were purchased with blood, priceless blood, divine blood, the blood of the Lamb of God, the Lord Jesus Christ's blood.

"Knowing that you were not redeemed with corruptible things, like silver or gold, from your aimless

conduct received by tradition from your fathers, but with the precious blood of Christ, as of a lamb without blemish and without spot" (1 Peter 1:18-19 NKJV).

"Or do you not know that your body is the temple of the Holy Spirit who is in you, whom you have from God, and you are not your own? For you were bought at a price; therefore glorify God in your body and in your spirit, which are God's" (1 Corinthians 6:19-20).

"And He took bread, gave thanks and broke it, and gave it to them, saying, "This is My body which is given for you; do this in remembrance of Me." Likewise He also took the cup after supper, saying, "This cup is the new covenant in My blood, which is shed for you." (Luke 22:19-20 NKJV).

Provision

Jesus has promised to take care of us, to clothe us, to provide a shelter for us and to never leave us nor forsake us.

"So why do you worry about clothing? Consider the lilies of the field, how they grow: they neither toil nor spin; and yet I say to you that even Solomon in all his glory was not arrayed like one of these. Now if God so clothes the grass of the field, which today is, and

tomorrow is thrown into the oven, will He not much more clothe you, O you of little faith?" (Matthew 6:28-30).

God knew that His people would break covenant and so He promised to make a new covenant with them.

> "Behold, the days are coming, says the Lord, when I will make a new covenant with the house of Israel and with the house of Judah—not according to the covenant that I made with their fathers in the day that I took them by the hand to lead them out of the land of Egypt, My covenant which they broke, though I was a husband to them, says the Lord. But this is the covenant that I will make with the house of Israel after those days, says the Lord: I will put My law in their minds, and write it on their hearts; and I will be their God, and they shall be My people. No more shall every man teach his neighbour, and every man his brother, saying, 'Know the Lord,' for they all shall know Me, from the least of them to the greatest of them, says the Lord. For I will forgive their iniquity, and their sin I will remember no more" (Jeremiah 31:31-34 NKJV).

The Ketubah or marriage contract, which was first promised to the house of Israel, was then opened up to "whosoever will". Non-Jews who at one time were strangers to God's covenant and promises could now enter in by the blood of the Lord

Jesus Christ and fully partake of His blessings. This included the blessing of Abraham as found in Galatians 3:29.

> *"And if you are Christ's, then you are Abraham's seed, and heirs according to the promise"* (Galatians 3:29 NKJV).

This new (marriage) covenant (we are now one with Christ) is built on better promises than the one God originally gave to the Jewish people at Mount Sinai.

> *"But now He has obtained a more excellent ministry, inasmuch as He is also Mediator of a better covenant, which was established on better promises"* (Hebrews 8:6 NKJV).

Intimacy

Through this covenant, Jesus promises to take God's law and place this on the inside of us, so that we might "know Him". The Hebrew word "to know Him" in Jeremiah 31:34, is the word 'yada' and it speaks of intimacy in relationship, to the deepest sense. This is the same Hebrew word for sexual intercourse. Found in Genesis 4:17, where it says, "Cane knew his wife and she conceived." God is calling us to the deepest, spiritual intimacy with Him, where deep calls unto deep.

> *"Deep calls unto deep at the noise of Your waterfalls; all Your waves and billows have gone over me"* (Psalm 42:7 NKJV).

Once again, out of this is birthed great fruitfulness. God wants to reveal to us deep and mighty things and I like to make a play on the word intimacy. "Into Me, you will see". The deeper we get into Jesus, the more we allow His Spirit and word to get into us, we will then see great and mighty things.

> *"But the people who know their God shall be strong, and carry out great exploits"* (Daniel 11:32b NKJV).

'Know' here is the same Hebrew word 'Yada' and through this knowing we will bring forth great exploits for the glory of God.

Although the Bride was selected for a Bridegroom, she had say in whether she was going to respond to the proposed marriage and enter into covenant with the Bridegroom. In Genesis 24:57-58 we read:

> *"So they said, "We will call the young woman and ask her personally." Then they called Rebekah and said to her, "Will you go with this man?"* (Genesis 24:57-58 NKJV).

Here we can see that even though Rebekah had brought Eleizer to her Father's house, when the marriage was discussed between her parents and Eleizer, before the final decision was made, they called Rebekah back in and asked her if she would go with Eleizer, back to Abraham's house. To which Rebekah replied "I will go", thereby consenting to the marriage.

Departure of the Bridegroom

In the Ancient Jewish custom, it was traditional that after the betrothal or engagement, the Bridegroom would leave his bride at her Father's house and he would go back to his Father's house to prepare a room, chamber or house built on his Father's property. He would then return up to a year later, after the place he had prepared was finished or complete, to bring his new bride. He comes with his wedding party to take his bride from her home and carry her back to his Father's house. They would then enter into the inner chamber and consummate the marriage. This would take traditionally seven days. After those seven days, they would come from the inner chamber and he would present himself and his bride to his friends and the world again.

In the book of Judges 14:12, we can see that after Samson married his wife, the marriage feast lasted seven days. This is one week and it is symbolic of the week or seven year period of time that we will spend with Jesus in heaven after the rapture or catching up of the church, until we come back with Him to reign and rule.

> *"Then Samson said to them, "Let me pose a riddle to you. If you can correctly solve and explain it to me within the seven days of the feast, then I will give you thirty linen garments and thirty changes of clothing"* (Judges 14:12 NKJV).

The inner chamber that the Bridegroom would prepare at his Father's house was in the Hebrew, known as 'Chadar'. Let's take a quick look at Psalm 45:10-11.

> *"Listen, O daughter, consider and incline your ear; Forget your own people also, and your father's house; So the King will greatly desire your beauty; Because He is your Lord, worship Him"* (Psalm 45:10-11 NKJV).

When Jesus spoke to His disciples in John 14:2-3, they knew He was talking in terms of marriage and painting the picture of the Ancient Jewish Wedding in their mind. It is very interesting also to note that the first miracle recorded that Jesus ever performed was at a wedding. The scripture declares, in this miracle, He showed forth His glory.

Jesus Promises to Come and Take Us Unto Himself

> *"In My Father's house are many mansions; if it were not so, I would have told you. I go to prepare a place for you. And if I go and prepare a place for you, I will come again and receive you to Myself; that where I am, there you may be also."* (John 14:2-3 NKJV).

God showed us the approximate time frame when Jesus would return for us in the book of Hosea 6:2-3.

> *"After two days He will revive us; on the third day He will raise us up, that we may live in His sight"* (Hosea 6:2 NKJV).

We have many other prophetic sign posts pointing to this time or season for The Rapture or catching away of the church as mentioned in previous chapters of this book.

In the customs of the Ancient Jewish Wedding, the Bridegroom would traditionally come at midnight or in the midnight hour. The Bride did not know the day or the hour that her Bridegroom would return, however, she knew the approximate time or season. The Bride would live in a state of readiness and preparedness for the return of her Bridegroom. She would keep the lamp burning so that if it was at midnight, she could easily race to the door of where she lived to meet him.

Traditionally, he would return with his party and they would come with burning torches, with singing and dancing and joy! There was a shout that would go out in the village of her tribe and family home. "Behold, the Bridegroom comes!" She would trim her lamp and rush out and he would catch her up in his arms and carry her back to his Father's house with great celebration and joy. They would then go into the inner chamber for seven days or one week, before he would present her to the world.

A Picture of the Return of Christ for His Prepared Church

"Then the kingdom of heaven shall be likened to ten virgins who took their lamps and went out to meet the bridegroom. Now five of them were wise, and five were foolish. Those who were foolish took their lamps and took no oil with them, but the wise took oil in their vessels with their lamps. But while the bridegroom was delayed, they all slumbered and slept. "And at midnight a cry was heard: 'Behold, the bridegroom is

coming; go out to meet him!' Then all those virgins arose and trimmed their lamps. And the foolish said to the wise, 'Give us some of your oil, for our lamps are going out.' But the wise answered, saying, 'No, lest there should not be enough for us and you; but go rather to those who sell, and buy for yourselves.' And while they went to buy, the bridegroom came, and those who were ready went in with him to the wedding; and the door was shut. "Afterward the other virgins came also, saying, 'Lord, Lord, open to us!' But he answered and said, 'Assuredly, I say to you, I do not know you.' "Watch therefore, for you know neither the day nor the hour in which the Son of Man is coming" (Matthew 25:1-13 NKJV).

In these verses, we see a beautiful analogy of Jesus returning for his church that is prepared, ready and waiting for Him. I see here that the five virgins that had oil in their lamps, which were burning bright, a picture of the Believers that are living for Jesus at the time of His return.

In Revelation 3:15-22, Jesus by His Holy Spirit, through the Apostle John, is talking to the Laodicean church. I believe this church is a representation of our modern day western affluent churches and believers. Jesus is bringing a strong word of correction leading to repentance, exhorting them to be ready, on fire and living for Him.

"I know your works, that you are neither cold nor hot: I wish you were either cold or hot. So then

because you are lukewarm, and neither cold nor hot, I will spue you out of my mouth. Because you say, I am rich, and increased with goods, and have need of nothing; and know not that you are wretched, and miserable, and poor, and blind, and naked: I counsel you to buy of me gold tried in the fire, that you may be rich; and white raiment, that you may be clothed, and that the shame of your nakedness do not appear; and anoint your eyes with eyesalve, that you may see. As many as I love, I rebuke and correct: be zealous therefore, and repent. Behold, I stand at the door, and knock: if any man hear my voice, and open the door, I will come in to him, and will dine with him, and he with me. To him that overcomes will I grant to sit with me in my throne, even as I also overcame, and am set down with my Father in his throne. He that hath an ear, let him hear what the Spirit says unto the churches" (Revelation 3:15-22).

After This

This leads us into Revelation 4:1.

"After these things I looked, and behold, a door standing open in heaven. And the first voice which I heard was like a trumpet speaking with me, saying, "Come up here, and I will show you things which must take place after this" (Revelation 4:1 NKJV).

As we read these portions of scripture, especially in the light of Matthew 25:1-13, we start to see a clear picture of The Rapture of the Church, which will then lead into the following events in the book of Revelation. Jesus also spoke of these events in the Gospels, which has been covered in previous chapters of this book. It is interesting to note that in Matthew 9:15, we see Jesus referring to His own rapture after His resurrection, where He was caught up into glory.

> *"And Jesus said to them, "Can the friends of the bridegroom mourn as long as the bridegroom is with them? But the days will come when the bridegroom will be taken away from them, and then they will fast"* (Matthew 9:15).

The disciples witnessed the rapture of Jesus, and the angels that appeared, told the disciples that in the same manner Jesus would come again. Jesus had instructed His disciples to go into all the world and preach the Gospel to every creature in all nations and then the end would come. What end was He referring to? I believe He was referring to the close of the Age of Grace, which would lead into Daniel's seventieth week or the last seven years, known as the Great Tribulation. When Jesus was caught up into glory, after fifty days the Holy Spirit was poured out on the Day of Pentecost and the Age of Grace or Church Age began. At the end of the Age of Grace, a two thousand year period of time, Jesus will return and catch His church or believers that are ready and looking for His coming up into His Father's house. Then God will pour out His final judgement on this planet, which will culminate with the Battle of Armageddon and the second coming of Jesus Christ. We will return with Jesus Christ at His second coming and we will reign with Him for one thousand years.

In the above verse of Matthew 9:15, you will notice Jesus finished His sentence with, and then His friends, the Believers, His disciples "will fast". Fasting is a discipline of our Christian walk. In my book on 'Fasting', I speak about the three great disciplines of the Christian faith, they are 'praying, giving and fasting'. You will find this in Matthew 6. Sometimes people ask me, "Shaun, how can I live Rapture Ready?" My reply to this is, as we have mentioned previously in this book, "Living life ready!" By that I mean, staying in a close fellowship and walk with the Lord, being open to the correction of the Holy Spirit. Keep your spirit well fed in the Word of God. Plan your life with goals and visions, like Jesus is not returning for a hundred years, but live your life like He is coming tomorrow. If you apply the three disciplines that Jesus spoke of in Matthew 6, and feed regularly on the Word you will be Rapture Ready.

"For where your treasure is, there your heart will be also" (Matthew 6:21 NKJV).

Jesus is coming back for those that are looking for Him, serving Him and are faithful. We all make mistakes or sin, and that is why I believe if you read Jesus' letters in Revelations 2 and 3 to the churches, you will see He praises and encourages His people, corrects and disciplines His people, and then rewards His people. He is always the loving Father who is forever wooing us back to Him, by His Holy Spirit reaching out and encouraging us to live for Him.

However, there will come a day when the trumpet will blow and the believers will distinctively hear his voice and we will be raptured. The door will close, the ready believers with their lamps burning, will go in the clouds of glory to heaven and then God will begin to pour out His judgement on the earth.

We see in the scripture in Revelation 4:1, the Apostle John says, that he looked and he saw a door opened in heaven and he heard a voice like a trumpet talking with him that said, "Come up here." This verse begins with the words (see above) "After this". After what? Well, chapter one of the book of Revelation, is a revelation of Jesus Christ, as the resurrected Almighty God. In chapters two and three, Jesus gives instruction, by His Spirit, through John to the seven churches. These churches are a representation of the church, down through the ages and in the world today. Jesus loves His church, He commends and praises His church for the good that it is doing. He corrects, disciplines His church for the errors of its way. He then encourages and promises great rewards to the Believers or churches that are open to and follow His correction and hold fast His word. I suggest that every Believer read Revelation chapter 2 and 3.

'After this', we see these words at the opening of Revelation chapter four. I believe, as it is written here, that when God finishes dealing with His church on the earth, it is raptured or caught up to heaven and is then found before the throne. We see here that John the Apostle, saw the open door in heaven, heard the trumpet blowing, discerned the sound and immediately found himself before the throne and Jesus Christ in glory. The Word says, that at midnight a cry will go forth, *"Behold the Bridegroom comes."* At the point of the Rapture, the trumpet of God will sound and the Believers will be caught up.

"For the Lord Himself will descend from heaven with a shout, with the voice of an archangel, and with the trumpet of God. And the dead in Christ will rise first.

Then we who are alive and remain shall be caught up together with them in the clouds to meet the Lord in the air. And thus we shall always be with the Lord. Therefore comfort one another with these words" (1 Thessalonians 4:16-18 NKJV).

The rest of chapter 4 and chapter 5 of the book of Revelation, describes the events taking place in the presence of God and before His throne. In verses 8, 9 and 10 of chapter 5, we see the church that is redeemed by Jesus' blood from all over the earth before the throne.

"Now when He had taken the scroll, the four living creatures and the twenty-four elders fell down before the Lamb, each having a harp, and golden bowls full of incense, which are the prayers of the saints. And they sang a new song, saying: You are worthy to take the scroll, and to open its seals; For You were slain, and have redeemed us to God by Your blood out of every tribe and tongue and people and nation, and have made us kings and priests to our God; And we shall reign on the earth" (Revelation 5:8-10 NKJV).

The obedient Believers that are living for Jesus at the time of His coming, are raptured up to heaven and are found before the throne, and then the events of the last seven years, begin to unfold from Revelation 6. God's judgement will be poured out over the next seven years, until the return of Christ at His second advent or coming, to usher in the one thousand years of peace.

The final great marriage will occur when God creates a new heaven and new earth, after His great white throne judgement. God will create a new heaven and a new earth, wherein dwells righteousness. The New Jerusalem will descend out of heaven as a bride prepared for her husband. We, led by Jesus, will triumphantly enter into this new city where God the Father himself shall be. From then on, we will go into the ages to come, living in the presence of the Father, Son and Holy Spirit, in the New Jerusalem upon the new earth in the new heavens. You can read of these events from Revelation 20:11 through to Revelation 22:21.

Scoffers

"Knowing this first: that scoffers will come in the last days, walking according to their own lusts" (2 Peter 3:3 NKJV).

The Jewish Bridegrooms would usually come for their Brides late at night, near the midnight hour, when shofars would blow breaking the silence of the night. The people would begin to cry, *"Behold the Bridegroom comes."* The reason that I believe so many of God's people are having visions and dreams of the Rapture and end-time events, is because it is a wakeup call for the church. In Matthew 25 or the verses we looked at above, all the ten virgins were asleep. Many of God's people have fallen asleep, concerning how close we are to the Rapture of the Church, the events of Daniel's seventieth week and the second coming of Christ.

God is waking us up out of our slumber and encouraging all His people all over the world to get back on fire for Him. Let's get back to our first love and start serving Jesus afresh again, winning souls for the Kingdom of God!

The Greater Glory

"Awake to righteousness, and do not sin; for some do not have the knowledge of God. I speak this to your shame" (1 Corinthians 15:34).

It is time to start feeding on God's word again. God has promised a last great revival before the Rapture.
"The glory of this latter house or temple shall be greater than the former,' says the Lord of hosts. 'And in this place I will give peace,' says the Lord of hosts" (Haggai 2:9 NKJV).

Remember, you are now the temple of God, after you become a born-again Believer (Christian).

"Do you not know that you are the temple of God and that the Spirit of God dwells in you?" (1 Corinthians 3:16 NKJV).

"Be diligent to present yourself approved to God, a worker who does not need to be ashamed, rightly dividing the word of truth" (2 Timothy 2:15 NKJV).

At the Rapture Jesus will come for His church, His Bride, to catch us away to heaven.

> "My beloved spoke, and said to me: "Rise up, my love, my fair one, and come away" (Song of Solomon 2:10 NKJV).

The Rapture as Seen in the Old Testament

> "Take Refuge from the Coming Judgement come, my people, enter your chambers, and shut your doors behind you; Hide yourself, as it were, for a little moment, until the indignation is past. For behold, the Lord comes out of His place to punish the inhabitants of the earth for their iniquity; The earth will also disclose her blood, and will no more cover her slain" (Isaiah 26:20-21 NKJV).

This is a picture of prophecy of Daniel's seventieth week, God's judgement being poured out. During this time, the church has entered into the inner chamber and the door is shut. We the Believers are with Christ in our glorious, heavenly home, while God pours out indignation and judgement on planet earth and those that are left behind.

Jesus Christ will come for us when His Father gives Him the permission to do so. We will hear a shout as well as the sound of the shofar, the trumpet of God! In Revelation 4:1-2, John heard this trumpet talking with Him and it called him up into glory, the third heaven. Here John, finds himself before the throne of God

> "After these things I looked, and behold, a door standing open in heaven. And the first voice which

I heard was like a trumpet speaking with me, saying, "Come up here, and I will show you things which must take place after this." Immediately I was in the Spirit; and behold, a throne set in heaven, and One sat on the throne" (Revelation 4:1-2 NKJV).

Discerning the Sound

John, the author or messenger of this Revelation, heard the trumpet blast and the words, "come up here". He had just noticed an open door. The Greek word used here for 'door' is the word 'Thura', it means by definition, a door. It is used as a door, or an opportunity. It comes from the root word origin; a door, doors, entrance, gate or gates. It has the urgency to rush in properly, that through which a rush is made.

In 1 Corinthians 15:52, we see this in action! Paul says, in a flash, in the twinkling of an eye, at the last trumpet we are all (Believers, both dead and alive) going to be changed. The word 'twinkling' in this scripture is the Greek word, 'atomos'. It means, "A moment of time that is so fast it cannot be divided into a faster time." It is indivisible, a moment, a split second, an instant, the shortest time possible.

"In a moment, in the twinkling of an eye, at the last trumpet. For the trumpet will sound, and the dead will be raised incorruptible, and we shall be changed" (1 Corinthians 15:52).

The door is an entrance, a way or a passage into, and as you can see it had opened in heaven. Now the Apostle John opens with the words 'after this'. This implies a change afterward. It is an active 'with', that looks towards the after effect, change or result, which is only defined by the context. We could use the word, "hereafter". In the context of what Jesus has just revealed to John, it's after, what the Spirit is finished saying to the churches on the earth. These churches represent all the churches spread throughout all the regions of the world.

Now let me summarize or explain this. Jesus Christ has just revealed himself to John as the Alpha and Omega; the Almighty God; the One who has risen from the dead, never to die again; the Lord of heaven and earth and the Lord and Saviour of His people, the churches.

His people are represented by the seven churches. John is to give this revelation to the servants of Jesus Christ, the disciples, plus those who believe in Jesus, from the Day of Pentecost, when the Church was born down through the last two thousand years, or the two days of grace.

This message is to go to the seven churches, which represent the entire church or body of Christ in the world today. This message of the Gospel, of who Jesus is, of the great salvation, available to all, and the final judgement of God, is to be preached by the born again believers, up to the Rapture of the Church.

After The Rapture, the Jewish timeline will start to tick off again. This timeline, as given to Daniel by Gabriel, was suspended at week sixty-nine, when Jesus was crucified. Remember, these are weeks of years. The last week or seven years (Jacob's trouble, Great Tribulation) will then count down from just after the Rapture until the Return of Christ, at the Great Tribulation. Jesus Christ will roar out of heaven like lightning, with His armies as the Almighty, all conquering God.

God and Judge of the Whole Earth

Now the revelation of Jesus, as the Son of God and our Lord and Saviour, has been carried into all the world for a witness, for the last two thousand years. With modern day communication, social media and technology, there has been an explosion of the Gospel now penetrating to the ends of the earth. Jesus himself said, when His Gospel has gone into all the world for a witness, the end would come.

I believe, in our day, we are seeing a convergence of many things, in our natural world, our political world and our economic world. The fulfilment of prophecy is happening before our eyes. This will lead to the catching up or the departure of the church at The Rapture. Jesus Christ is then revealed as the Almighty God and Judge of the whole earth from heaven.

When we are born again we pass from spiritual death to spiritual life.

> *"I am crucified with Christ: nevertheless I live; yet not I, but Christ lives in me: and the life which I now live in the flesh I live by the faith of the Son of God, who loved me, and gave himself for me"* (Galatians 2:20).

"And as it is appointed unto men once to die, but after this the judgment" (Hebrews 9:27).

"The ones He loved and loves and washed from their sins with His own blood. He made them Kings and priests unto God and His Father" (Revelation 1: 5b-6a).

As Christians, we are to reckon ourselves dead, crucified with Christ, yet alive! Raised to life with Him, never to spiritually die again. Water baptism is a beautiful picture of this revelation!

For further information on water baptism, refer to my book *'Life Changing Principles for Victorious Living'*.

Judgements

The time of the Great Tribulation, Daniel's seventieth week, is the world's judgement. It's finalized with Jesus Christ judging the nations, along with the Anti-Christ and False Prophet. Satan himself will also be at this time thrown into the bottomless pit for one thousand years. He remains there during the millennial reign of Jesus Christ. Until He is let loose again for one final time, that finishes with the Great White Throne judgement of God.

Communion is where we, the Church or Believers, during this dispensation are judged. It is a self-examination or self-judgement to realign ourselves with God and His Word. If we have backslidden or messed up in any way, we can repent and return to Jesus, His Word and Spirit, our first love.

This is why we are exhorted so much through the Word, by Paul, others and Jesus himself, to watch and pray. God wants us to live by faith in His grace, not bearing grudges, but forgiving one another and encouraging each other. We are to live in an attitude of gratitude, watching and prayer, staying sober and alert, as we see that great day of His coming approach. If we sin, we are to repent, by forsaking our sins and getting back in love and on fire for Jesus again.

We are to judge or examine ourselves to see if we be in the faith. Jesus is looking for faith and faithfulness.

> *"I tell you that he will avenge them speedily. Nevertheless when the Son of man cometh, shall he find faith on the earth?"* (Luke 18:8).

> *"For if we would judge ourselves, we should not be judged. But when we are judged, we are disciplined of the Lord, that we should not be condemned with the world"* (1 Corinthians 11:31-32).

For more information of this, please refer my book, 'Life Changing Principles for Victorious Living', the chapter on Communion.

The Revelation of Jesus Christ

> *"And from Jesus Christ, the faithful witness, the firstborn from the dead, and the ruler over the kings of the earth. To Him who loved us and washed us from*

our sins in His own blood, and has made us kings and priests to His God and Father, to Him be glory and dominion forever and ever. Amen" (Revelation 1:5-6 NKJV).

The book of Revelation, is a book where mysteries are being revealed, to John the Apostle. John is then told to reveal them to the servants of Jesus Christ.

"The Revelation of Jesus Christ, which God gave Him to show His servants—things which must shortly take place. And He sent and signified it by His angel to His servant John" (Revelation 1:1).

Do Not Seal Up These Words

In Revelation 22:10 (the last chapter of Revelation), we read *"And he said to me, "Do not seal the words of the prophecy of this book, for the time is at hand."*

Unlike the book of Daniel, where in chapter 12: 9, Daniel was told that the words are sealed until the time of the end.

"And he said, "Go your way, Daniel, for the words are closed up and sealed till the time of the end" (Daniel 12:9).

The words of the book of Revelation are not to be sealed but to be given to the churches, that is you and I. I believe we are in the time of the end, a period of time just before the Rapture of the Church and the beginning of the last seven years, which will culminate with the second coming of Jesus Christ.

In Revelation 1, Jesus has revealed himself as the Alpha and Omega. And again in Revelation 22:13, Jesus reveals himself as the Alpha and the Omega.

> *"And behold, I am coming quickly, and My reward is with Me, to give to every one according to his work. I am the Alpha and the Omega, the Beginning and the End, the First and the Last." Blessed are those who do His commandments, that they may have the right to the tree of life, and may enter through the gates into the city"* (Revelation 22:12-14 NKJV).

Now let's explain what John was referring to in Revelation 4:1, when he "after this". In Revelation 2 & 3, the Holy Spirit speaks expressly to the churches bringing praise, correction, instruction and ultimate reward for submitting to the will of God and getting back into intimate fellowship with Jesus.

The Close of the Age of Grace

After the church age is fulfilled, and God finishes speaking to the churches on the earth, the Church is caught into Glory. A door opens in heaven and a trumpet sounds the trump of God. This is not the trumpets that the angels blow during the tribulation, when God's judgements are poured out into the earth (refer to Revelation 8:1), but this trumpet here is the trumpet that the Apostle Paul refers to in 1 Thessalonians 4:16 & 17.

> *"For the Lord Himself will descend from heaven with a shout, with the voice of an archangel, and with the trumpet of God. And the dead in Christ will rise first. Then we who are alive and remain shall be caught up together with them in the clouds to meet the Lord in the air. And thus we shall always be with the Lord"* (1 Thessalonians 4:16-17).

It is interesting to note that in 1 Corinthians 13:3, that prophecies will pass away, but tongues will cease. These are two different Greek words. This is because tongues, is a peculiar gift for the Church Age only. Tongues was given as empowerment to the church by the Holy Spirit at Pentecost. It was given, in order that the church could edify itself, strengthen itself and build itself up in the holy faith given to us as Believers by Jesus Christ. Tongues will cease at The Rapture, but prophecy will go on until it is all fulfilled and passes away, with the beginning of the new heaven and new earth.

> *"Love never fails. But whether there are prophecies, they will fail; whether there are tongues, they will cease; whether there is knowledge, it will vanish away"* (1 Corinthians 13:8).

> *"But ye, beloved, building up yourselves on your most holy faith, praying in the Holy Spirit"* (Jude 20).

For more information of this, please refer my book, 'Life Changing Principles for Victorious Living', the chapter on 'Praying in Tongues'.

Believers Will Hear the Trump of God

Christians, hear that trumpet blast, the same one that John heard. They see the open door and they hear or discern what the trumpet sound says, which is, *"Come up here"*. Do you remember when Jesus called Lazareth from the grave? Jesus said, *"Lazareth arise and come forth!"* This time Jesus is not calling one dead man out of a tomb, but He is calling the dead in Christ, out of their tombs, along with all the living Believers up into heaven, with Him.

This is why from verse 2 of Revelation 4, John finds himself before the throne of God and who do we see there with him? We see the church before the throne of God. In Revelation 5:9 & 10, please read slowly Revelation 5:5-12.

> *"But one of the elders said to me, "Do not weep. Behold, the Lion of the tribe of Judah, the Root of David, has prevailed to open the scroll and to loose its seven seals." And I looked, and behold, in the midst of the throne and of the four living creatures, and in the midst of the elders, stood a Lamb as though it had been slain, having seven horns and seven eyes, which are the seven Spirits of God sent out into all the earth. Then He came and took the scroll out of the right hand of Him who sat on the throne. Now when He had taken the scroll, the four living creatures and the twenty-four elders fell down before the Lamb, each having a harp, and golden bowls full of incense, which are the prayers of the saints. And they sang*

a new song, saying: "You are worthy to take the scroll, and to open its seals; for You were slain, and have redeemed us to God by Your blood out of every tribe and tongue and people and nation, and have made us kings and priests to our God; And we shall reign on the earth." Then I looked, and I heard the voice of many angels around the throne, the living creatures, and the elders; and the number of them was ten thousand times ten thousand, and thousands of thousands, saying with a loud voice: "Worthy is the Lamb who was slain to receive power and riches and wisdom, and strength and honor and glory and blessing!" (Revelation 5:5-12 NKJV).

The Raptured Church Before the Throne

You will notice that the church sings a song and part of the words are as above, you have made us Kings and Priests unto our God and we shall reign on the earth. Here we see a definite and strong picture, revelation given to John by the Lord Jesus Christ Himself. Once again, after God finishes dealing with the church on the earth, they are caught up through an open door/passage way into heaven and are singing and worshipping before the throne of God and the Lamb of God, the Lord Jesus Christ Himself. Declaring that they will, in the future (this will be after the seven year tribulation) reign with Jesus on the earth. We see in verse 5 above, that Jesus takes the book out of God's hand and He starts to loose the seven seals, around the book.

Revelation chapters 6 and 7, reveals what begins to take place on the earth as Jesus opens the seals. It begins with the releasing of the four horsemen of the Apocalypse. Once again, I want you to take notice as to where the church is when the Apocalypse is being released on the earth as per Revelation chapters 6 & 7. They are safe with Jesus before the throne in the heavenly realms of glory.

The first time Jesus comes for His church, He comes with the trumpet of God in the clouds and all Believers, both dead and alive are caught up into that cloud in the air and transported back to where Jesus has come from.

> *"Let not your heart be troubled; you believe in God, believe also in Me. In My Father's house are many mansions; if it were not so, I would have told you. I go to prepare a place for you. And if I go and prepare a place for you, I will come again and receive you to Myself; that where I am, there you may be also. And where I go you know, and the way you know"* (John 14:1-4 NKJV).

Here in this verse we see, Jesus promises to come back and take us to the place He has prepared for us. This happens at the Rapture. It's a mansion, a special place within His Father's house. A careful study of Acts 1:8-11 will reveal the Rapture of the Lord Jesus Christ when he was taken up into heaven and a cloud received Him out of their sight. The angels told the disciples that this is how Jesus would come back for them.

He will come in the clouds of the air to catch up the church, His disciples, His faithful followers and take them back to the heavenly mansions and realms of glory in His Father's house.

Caught Up in the Clouds

"Now when He had spoken these things, while they watched, He was taken up, and a cloud received Him out of their sight. And while they looked steadfastly toward heaven as He went up, behold, two men stood by them in white apparel, who also said, "Men of Galilee, why do you stand gazing up into heaven? This same Jesus, who was taken up from you into heaven, will so come in like manner as you saw Him go into heaven" (Acts 1:9-11 NKJV).

At the Rapture of the church, Jesus' feet do not touch the ground. He comes in the clouds of the air. Only the dead in Christ, who are raised and the living Believers, get to see Him. 1 Corinthians 15:51 & 52 calls this a mystery. Paul reveals this mystery to us, the Believers, for our enlightenment and empowerment. In verse 18 of 1 Thessalonians 4, he tells us to comfort one another with these words. He goes on and tells us in verses 1 and 2 of 1 Thessalonians 5, that Jesus will come as a thief in the night.

"But concerning the times and the seasons, brethren, you have no need that I should write to you. For you yourselves know perfectly that the day of the Lord so comes as a thief in the night" (1 Thessalonians 5:1-2 NKJV).

Jesus reiterates this himself in Revelation 16:15.

> *"Behold, I am coming as a thief. Blessed is he who watches, and keeps his garments, lest he walk naked and they see his shame"* (Revelation 16:15).

Pearls of Great Price

When a thief breaks into a house, he comes for the valuables, the silver, the gold, the good stuff. Jesus is coming in the midnight hour, as a thief in the night for the pearls of great price. That is you and I, the blood washed, born of the Spirit, Believers that are walking in fellowship with the Spirit and the Word. He is coming for His redeemed Kings and Priests that He has redeemed by His own blood, washing them from their sins.

> *"Again, the kingdom of heaven is like unto a merchant man, seeking goodly pearls: Who, when he had found one pearl of great price, went and sold all that he had, and bought it"* (Matthew 13:45-46).

At the Rapture, His feet do not touch the ground and only the Believers will see Him.

At His second coming, Jesus comes with the clouds and every eye will see Him and all the people from all nations of the earth, at that time, will weep and cry because of Him.

> *"Behold, He is coming with clouds, and every eye will see Him, even they who pierced Him. And all the*

tribes of the earth will mourn because of Him. Even so, Amen" (Revelation 1:7 NKJV).

We will come back with Jesus to the earth at His second coming to reign and rule with Him for one thousand years. This will be after the seven years of tribulation and at the battle of Armageddon where Jesus will annihilate the anti-Christ and obliterate his armies.

Return of the Bridegroom

Here we see Jesus Christ the Almighty God, returning to the earth at His second coming as the Judge of the whole earth.

> "Now I saw heaven opened, and behold, a white horse. And He who sat on him was called Faithful and True, and in righteousness He judges and makes war. His eyes were like a flame of fire, and on His head were many crowns. He had a name written that no one knew except Himself. He was clothed with a robe dipped in blood, and His name is called The Word of God. And the armies in heaven, clothed in fine linen, white and clean, followed Him on white horses. Now out of His mouth goes a sharp sword, that with it He should strike the nations. And He Himself will rule them with a rod of iron. He Himself treads the winepress of the fierceness and wrath of Almighty God. And He has on His robe and on His thigh a name written: KING OF KINGS AND LORD OF LORDS" (Revelation 19:11-16 NKJV).

"For as the lightning comes from the east and flashes to the west, so also will the coming of the Son of Man be" (Matthew 24:27 NKJV).

Let us prepare our hearts for His coming, let us look up because as the Bible says, *"Our redemption draws near."*

The Huppah

The second half of the Ancient Jewish Wedding ceremony, 'Huppah', as it is referred to in the Hebrew, is also called the 'Home Taking'. In the wedding ceremony the 'Huppah' refers to both the ceremony itself and the actual bridal canopy that covers the bridal couple. The original meaning of 'Huppah' was 'room' or 'covering'. The 'Huppah' of ancient times was a special room built in the Bridegroom's Father's house. Jesus told us, in my Father's house are many mansions and I am going to there to prepare a place for you. Then He said, *"I will come again to receive or take you to myself, that where I am you may be also."*

That my friend, is The Rapture and the catching up of the Church. The 'Huppah' is also mentioned in the Bible verses below.

> *"Which is like a bridegroom coming out of his chamber, and rejoices like a strong man to run its race"* (Psalm 19:5).

Notice the Bridegroom comes out of His chamber.

> "Blow the trumpet in Zion, consecrate a fast, call a sacred assembly. Gather the people, sanctify the congregation, assemble the elders, gather the children and nursing babes; Let the bridegroom go out from his chamber, and the bride from her dressing room" (Joel 2:15-16 NKJV).

First of all, Jesus will come for us at the Rapture and take us back to heaven with Him. Then after seven years, He will come back to liberate Israel and the faithful remnant of His people Israel. He will then judge the nations, then setup His millennial reign for one thousand years.

> "Assemble and come, all you nations, and gather together all around. Cause Your mighty ones to go down there, O Lord. "Let the nations be wakened, and come up to the Valley of Jehoshaphat; For there I will sit to judge all the surrounding nations. Put in the sickle, for the harvest is ripe. Come, go down; For the winepress is full, the vats overflow—for their wickedness is great." Multitudes, multitudes in the valley of decision! For the day of the Lord is near in the valley of decision. The sun and moon will grow dark, and the stars will diminish their brightness. The Lord also will roar from Zion, and utter His voice from Jerusalem; The heavens and earth will shake; but the Lord will be a shelter for His people, and the strength of the children of Israel. "So you shall know that I am the Lord your God, dwelling in Zion

My holy mountain. Then Jerusalem shall be holy, and no aliens shall ever pass through her again." And it will come to pass in that day that the mountains shall drip with new wine, the hills shall flow with milk, and all the brooks of Judah shall be flooded with water; A fountain shall flow from the house of the Lord and water the Valley of Acacias. "Egypt shall be a desolation, and Edom a desolate wilderness, because of violence against the people of Judah, for they have shed innocent blood in their land. But Judah shall abide forever, and Jerusalem from generation to generation. For I will acquit them of the guilt of bloodshed, whom I had not acquitted; for the Lord dwells in Zion" (Joel 3:11-21).

These scriptures above, occur when Jesus comes back at His second coming. His feet will touch down on the Mount of Olivet, causing a great earthquake.

A Great Earthquake

"Behold, the day of the Lord is coming, and your spoil will be divided in your midst. For I will gather all the nations to battle against Jerusalem; The city shall be taken, the houses rifled, and the women ravished. Half of the city shall go into captivity, but the remnant of the people shall not be cut off from the city. Then the Lord will go forth and fight against those nations, as He fights in the day of battle. And in that day His

feet will stand on the Mount of Olives, which faces Jerusalem on the east. And the Mount of Olives shall be split in two, from east to west, making a very large valley; Half of the mountain shall move toward the north and half of it toward the south. Then you shall flee through My mountain valley, for the mountain valley shall reach to Azal. Yes, you shall flee as you fled from the earthquake in the days of Uzziah king of Judah. Thus the Lord my God will come, and all the saints with You" (Zechariah 14:1-5 NKJV).

Notice verse five here, when Jesus comes to judge the nations, that have gathered against Israel at the battle of Armageddon. Verse five says, *"The Lord my God will come and all His Saints will come with Him."* When Jesus comes back to reign and rule for a thousand years, we are coming back with Him to reign and rule the earth under Him, under His power and authority. This is because seven years prior to this, Jesus caught us up into heaven.

Logic says, how can we come back with Jesus to reign and rule, if we haven't at a prior time left the earth!

The Bridegroom, in the Ancient Jewish Wedding, would always arrive at the 'Huppah' first. He would then welcome His B ride to the place He had prepared for her. The Bride and Groom would greet the guests gathered at His Father's house and then escort his Bride to the bridal chamber where they would be alone for seven days, during which time the marriage was consummated. The best-man or friend of the Bridegroom would wait outside the wedding chamber to hear the voice of the Bridegroom call out to him and tell him the marriage was consummated. Then all of the guests began a weeklong celebration! As you are aware, from previous chapters, The Great Tribulation on earth is one week or seven years long according to Daniel's prophecy.

"He who has the bride is the bridegroom; but the friend of the bridegroom, who stands and hears him, rejoices greatly because of the bridegroom's voice. Therefore this joy of mine is fulfilled" (John 3:29 NKJV).

The Rapture Mystery Revealed

"Behold, I tell you a mystery: We shall not all sleep, but we shall all be changed— in a moment, in the twinkling of an eye, at the last trumpet. For the trumpet will sound, and the dead will be raised incorruptible, and we shall be changed. For this corruptible must put on incorruption, and this mortal must put on immortality. So when this corruptible has put on incorruption, and this mortal has put on immortality, then shall be brought to pass the saying that is written: "Death is swallowed up in victory." "O Death, where is your sting? O Hades, where is your victory?" (1 Corinthians 15:51-55 NKJV).

In a twinkling of the eye, at the blast of the trumpet of God and the shout of the voice of the Archangel, who sounds, "Come up here!" We shall be raptured. The dead in Christ first and then we which are alive and remain, will all be one together with Jesus, physically alive, changed from corruption to incorruption, from mortal to immortal by the power of the Holy Spirit. We shall be one with Jesus, exactly like He is. We would have put on our resurrected, eternal new bodies, never to die again! The marriage will be consummated, and we will go to heaven with Jesus for one week, seven years to celebrate and to train for reigning on the earth. We will then return with Jesus as part of the armies of heaven to watch Jesus destroy the False Prophet, the Anti-Christ and all those that oppose Christ and His Kingdom.

After the battle of Armageddon in the Valley of Meggido (Jezreel), Jesus will sit to judge the nations in the Valley of Jehoshaphat. Possibly a newly formed valley, caused by the great earthquake that splits the Mount of Olives, when Jesus the Almighty God, Alpha and Omega puts His foot back down physically on the ground. (For further study on this please read Zechariah 14:1-21).

> *"For as in Adam all die, even so in Christ all shall be made alive. But each one in his own order: Christ the firstfruits, afterward those who are Christ's at His coming. Then comes the end, when He delivers the kingdom to God the Father, when He puts an end to all rule and all authority and power. For He must reign till He has put all enemies under His feet. The last enemy that will be destroyed is death. For "He has put all things under His feet." But when He says "all things are put under Him," it is evident that He*

who put all things under Him is excepted. Now when all things are made subject to Him, then the Son Himself will also be subject to Him who put all things under Him, that God may be all in all" (1 Corinthians 15:22-28 NKJV).

We can see from the above scriptures that in Christ, all shall be made alive. This will take place at The Rapture of the Church. We can see that after this, the end comes, this will be after the seven years of The Great Tribulation, Daniel's seventieth week. During the one thousand years of Christ's millennial reign, physical death will be banished from the earth.

The Dead in Christ Shall Live

"Your dead shall live; together with my dead body they shall arise. Awake and sing, you who dwell in dust; For your dew is like the dew of herbs, and the earth shall cast out the dead. Take Refuge from the coming Judgment come, my people, enter your chambers, and shut your doors behind you; Hide yourself, as it were, for a little moment, until the indignation is past. For behold, the Lord comes out of His place to punish the inhabitants of the earth for their iniquity; The earth will also disclose her blood, and will no more cover her slain" (Isaiah 26:19-21 NKJV).

In the above verses, we have a beautiful picture from the Old Testament of the resurrection of Jesus, The Rapture of the Church, when the dead in Christ rise first and we which are alive at that time are caught up together with Him into glory. We see the coming great judgement of God during the time of the Great Tribulation. The scripture declares that we, God's people, will be safe because he has commanded us to enter in and He has shut the door behind us. During this time, which is seven years long, God will come to punish the inhabitants of the earth for their wickedness. In the above verse notice the phrase, *"the earth shall cast out the dead."*

Paul calls The Rapture a mystery, He declares Christ is risen from the dead and the first fruits of them that are asleep. He says, that this will happen in a moment, in the twinkling of an eye, at the last trump. (Refer to above verses). Then in 1 Thessalonians 4 he tells us, that when Jesus descends from heaven with the voice of the Archangel and the trumpet of God, the dead in Christ will rise first and those Believers living at that time will be caught up into the air with them, and we will ever be with the Lord. This is a great mystery and will be fulfilled at The Rapture.

In 1 Thessalonians 5: 1-11, we see further great insight into this time and in verse 11, we are instructed to comfort one another and edify each other. This is because of verse 2, where we see Jesus will come as a "thief in the night". This is not a reference to the second coming, because at the second coming, every eye will see Him. Only the Believers that are ready and waiting, looking for His coming will see Him when He comes as a thief in the night, and go with Him.

"But concerning the times and the seasons, brethren, you have no need that I should write to you. For you

yourselves know perfectly that the day of the Lord so comes as a thief in the night. For when they say, "Peace and safety!" then sudden destruction comes upon them, as labor pains upon a pregnant woman. And they shall not escape. But you, brethren, are not in darkness, so that this Day should overtake you as a thief. You are all sons of light and sons of the day. We are not of the night nor of darkness. Therefore let us not sleep, as others do, but let us watch and be sober. For those who sleep, sleep at night, and those who get drunk are drunk at night. But let us who are of the day be sober, putting on the breastplate of faith and love, and as a helmet the hope of salvation. For God did not appoint us to wrath, but to obtain salvation through our Lord Jesus Christ, who died for us, that whether we wake or sleep, we should live together with Him. Therefore comfort each other and edify one another, just as you also are doing" (1 Thessalonians 5:1-11 NKJV).

Notice in the above verses, the term "they shall not escape". It goes on to say, but you Believers are not of the darkness "but are children of the light and the children of the day." So therefore, let us not sleep as do others, but let us watch and be sober. (Clear presence of mind, clear judgement). It tells us to keep on the breastplate of faith and love and the helmet of the hope of salvation, because God has not appointed us to wrath. God has not appointed us to the day of His great judgement, but to obtain salvation, through our Lord Jesus Christ.

> "Now, brethren, concerning the coming of our Lord Jesus Christ and our gathering together to Him, we ask you, not to be soon shaken in mind or troubled, either by spirit or by word or by letter, as if from us, as though the day of Christ had come" (2 Thessalonians 2:1-2 NKJV).

Paul, here, is further building on the revelation he has released in 1 Thessalonians, especially in chapter 4:13, where he tells us that he would not have us be ignorant concerning those that are dead, or asleep in Christ, that we sorrow not as others that have no hope. The dead in Christ will rise at the Rapture. All the rest of the dead, down through the ages, will not be raised to life until after the one thousand year millennial reign. All the rest of the people that have ever lived will then be raised to life to go before the great white throne judgement of God. For further understanding and reading please read Revelation 20: 1-6.

> "Then I saw an angel coming down from heaven, having the key to the bottomless pit and a great chain in his hand. He laid hold of the dragon, that serpent of old, who is the Devil and Satan, and bound him for a thousand years; and he cast him into the bottomless pit, and shut him up, and set a seal on him, so that he should deceive the nations no more till the thousand years were finished. But after these things he must be released for a little while. And I saw thrones, and they sat on them, and judgment was committed to them. Then I saw the souls of those who had been beheaded

for their witness to Jesus and for the word of God, who had not worshipped the beast or his image, and had not received his mark on their foreheads or on their hands. And they lived and reigned with Christ for a thousand years. But the rest of the dead did not live again until the thousand years were finished. This is the first resurrection. Blessed and holy is he who has part in the first resurrection. Over such the second death has no power, but they shall be priests of God and of Christ, and shall reign with Him a thousand years" (Revelation 20:1-6 NKJV).

The first resurrection includes, the Saints that were raised from the dead, when Jesus was first raised from the dead.

"And the graves were opened; and many bodies of the saints who had fallen asleep were raised; and coming out of the graves after His resurrection, they went into the holy city and appeared to many" (Matthew 27:52-53 NKJV).

The born-again Believers, the dead in Christ raised at The Rapture, the Saints that are saved and killed for the witness of Jesus, and the Word of God during the tribulation, we will all reign and rule with Jesus for a thousand years and then sit on thrones as Priests of God and Christ. God then presides over the final judgement of Satan and the rest of the dead, whose names are not found written in the Book of Life. Those not found written in the Book of Life will be cast into the Lake of Fire. Please refer to Revelation 20:7-15.

In 2 Thessalonians 2, if you look at the context, Paul is not talking about the second coming, but rather The Rapture of the Church, when we are gathered together unto Jesus. He specifically says, he doesn't want the church to be troubled or shaken in their minds or their spirits. He had already told the Believers in the previous letter to stay clear, sober, focused in mind. He goes on to say in verse 3 and 4, that we are not to let anyone deceive us, that the day of Christ is at hand!

The Day of Christ, is the second coming of Jesus that occurs at the end of the Great Tribulation, when He will judge the nations. Paul wants to give the Believers peace and confidence that before that day occurs, which is at the end of the Great Tribulation, Daniel's seventieth week, the Rapture will occur first. Then the Anti-Christ will be revealed and the last seven years will tick off the Jewish time clock.

Now as explained previously, the day of Christ is a thousand years long and starts with the return of Christ at the Battle of Armageddon. Remember, we will return with Jesus. Here are the two verses that confuse many Christians, please read, the scriptures below and then I will expand and explain.

> *"Let no one deceive you by any means; for that Day will not come unless the falling away comes first, and the man of sin is revealed, the son of perdition, who opposes and exalts himself above all that is called God or that is worshipped, so that he sits as God in the temple of God, showing himself that he is God"* (2 Thessalonians 2:3-4 NKJV).

The term *"for that day shall not come, except there come a falling away first and the man of sin* (the Anti-Christ) *is revealed, the Son of Perdition"*, is not a reference to great Apostasy or backsliding. Here, the word 'Apostasy' can also be correctly interpreted in a positive sense. We know that from Paul's writing, he is delivering a word of comfort. In verse context, chapter context and context with 1 & 2 Thessalonians, where Paul exhorts us, comfort one another, with these words, this term here can, in the Greek context be accurately translated, as "the departure of the church".

A footnote, in the Amplified version of the Bible, at the bottom of this scripture explains this. It says Apostasy, in this context, can be rendered *"the departure of the church"*.

Now in 2 Thessalonians 2:5-17, we can read the rest of Paul's revelation or revealed mystery.

> *"Do you not remember that when I was still with you I told you these things? And now you know what is restraining, that he may be revealed in his own time. For the mystery of lawlessness is already at work; only He who now restrains will do so until He is taken out of the way. And then the lawless one will be revealed, whom the Lord will consume with the breath of His mouth and destroy with the brightness of His coming. The coming of the lawless one is according to the working of Satan, with all power, signs, and lying wonders, and with all unrighteous deception among those who perish, because they*

did not receive the love of the truth, that they might be saved. And for this reason God will send them strong delusion, that they should believe the lie, that they all may be condemned who did not believe the truth but had pleasure in unrighteousness. But we are bound to give thanks to God always for you, brethren beloved by the Lord, because God from the beginning chose you for salvation through sanctification by the Spirit and belief in the truth, to which He called you by our gospel, for the obtaining of the glory of our Lord Jesus Christ. Therefore, brethren, stand fast and hold the traditions which you were taught, whether by word or our epistle. Now may our Lord Jesus Christ Himself, and our God and Father, who has loved us and given us everlasting consolation and good hope by grace, comfort your hearts and establish you in every good word and work" (2 Thessalonians 2:5-17 NKJV).

Paul says in the above verses, that we know (Believers know) what withholds or restrains and restricts the Anti-Christ until he is revealed in his time. God has allotted seven years, Daniel's seventieth week for the Anti-Christ to operate in His fullest capacity. This is when he will be possessed by Satan himself and demand the worship of all people of all nations.

Verse seven tells us that the Anti-Christ Spirit is already at work, only he who restrains him will continue to restrain him until he is taken out of the way. Verse eight then says, then this wicked one will be revealed and Jesus Christ will destroy him at His second coming. It goes on to say that his power is the power of Satan and he works lying signs and wonders and brings strong deception onto peoples' minds. They then start believing his lies. This spirit of deception and delusion is at work in these last days and Jesus warns that it will even try deceiving the very elect of God.

The Authority of the Name of Jesus

The "he" that the scripture is referring to here, as we all know is the church, empowered by the Holy Spirit, through the Word of God, exercising the authority of the Name of Jesus.

> *"Then the seventy returned with joy, saying, "Lord, even the demons are subject to us in Your name." And He said to them, "I saw Satan fall like lightning from heaven"* (Luke 10:17-18 NKJV).

The church, through the authority of the name of Jesus Christ, has the power to cast out devils, restrain the Anti-Christ and pull down the works of Satan.

> *"Behold, I give you the authority to trample on serpents and scorpions, and over all the power of the enemy, and nothing shall by any means hurt you. Nevertheless do not rejoice in this, that the spirits are subject to you, but rather rejoice because your names are written in heaven"* (Luke 10:19-20 NKJV).

> *"Assuredly, I say to you, whatever you bind on earth will be bound in heaven, and whatever you loose on earth will be loosed in heaven. "Again I say to you that if two of you agree on earth concerning anything that they ask, it will be done for them by My Father in heaven"* (Matthew 18:18-19 NKJV).

The church has the power to bind and loose. Satan will not reveal his Anti-Christ until after the departure of the church at The Rapture. This is why Paul reiterates, through Thessalonians 1 & 2, that we can comfort one another with these words, *"We have not been appointed to the day, time or season of God's wrath and judgement. But instead, we have been appointed to obtain salvation, to 'The Blessing of Abraham' that includes The Rapture of the Church."*

The Gates of Hell

Jesus said, *"The gates of hell themselves will not prevail against his church."* We have been born-again to win, to overcome, to prevail and to reign and rule in life through Jesus Christ. During the Dispensation of Grace, until the great catching up of the church, we are to bind Satan's power and take the gospel into all the world, with a demonstration of God's power to all creation. Jesus then states that after the church has finished it's assignment the end shall come. Please refer to Matthew 28:18-20 & Mark 16:15-20.

One of the signs of Jesus' empowerment of a Believer's life is that they can cast out devils. After the church is taken out of the way, at The Rapture, Satan will endeavour to bring in His

Kingdom under the rulership of the Anti-Christ. However, during this time, God will go forth and pour out his judgement.

> *"The great day of the Lord is near; It is near and hastens quickly. The noise of the day of the Lord is bitter; there the mighty men shall cry out. That day is a day of wrath, a day of trouble and distress, a day of devastation and desolation, a day of darkness and gloominess, a day of clouds and thick darkness, a day of trumpet and alarm, against the fortified cities, and against the high towers. "I will bring distress upon men, and they shall walk like blind men, because they have sinned against the Lord; Their blood shall be poured out like dust, and their flesh like refuse."* (Zephaniah 1:14-17 NKJV).

We can see in the above verse, the final day and time of judgement during Daniel's seventieth week, which is also known as the Great Tribulation. This will culminate with Jesus Christ judging the nations, before we enter into His millennial reign.

Nahum's Account

We can see here Nahum's account of the tribulation and the Battle of Armageddon before the one thousand years reign of peace. We will look at another prophetic scripture in Nahum chapter 2:4, to see a prophetic picture of the time frame in which this occurs.

> *"God is jealous, and the Lord avenges; God's Wrath on His Enemies, God is jealous, and the Lord avenges; The Lord avenges and is furious. The Lord will take vengeance on His adversaries, and He reserves wrath for His enemies; The Lord is slow to anger and great in power, and will not at all acquit the wicked. The Lord has His way in the whirlwind and in the storm, and the clouds are the dust of His feet. He rebukes the sea and makes it dry, and dries up all the rivers. Bashan and Carmel wither, and the flower of Lebanon wilts. The mountains quake before Him, the hills melt, and the earth heaves at His presence, Yes, the world and all who dwell in it. Who can stand before His indignation? And who can endure the fierceness of His anger? His fury is poured out like fire, and the rocks are thrown down by Him. The Lord is good, a stronghold in the day of trouble; And He knows those who trust in Him. But with an overflowing flood, He will make an utter end of its place, and darkness will pursue His enemies. What do you conspire against the Lord? He will make an utter end of it. Affliction will not rise up a second time"* (Nahum 1:2-9 NKJV).

In the verses above, we can plainly see the time of great tribulation and what it will be like during this time on the earth, and how God will make an utter end of the enemies of righteousness, at that time. We can also see in verse seven that at this time, when God is pouring out His judgement, the righteousness and those that have put their trust in Him are safe! God is a stronghold in the day of trouble, The Great Tribulation.

Army of Two Hundred Million

"The shields of his mighty men are made red, the valiant men are in scarlet. The chariots come with flaming torches in the day of his preparation, and the spears are brandished. The chariots rage in the streets, they jostle one another in the broad roads; They seem like torches, they run like lightning" (Nahum 2:3-4 NKJV).

The bible speaks about an army that will come against Israel from the north. It also speaks about an army of two hundred million soldiers that will come out of the East. We can see this army in Revelation 9:16.

It is interesting to note that both China and Russia's armies are symbolized by the colour red.

"Now the number of the army of the horsemen was two hundred million; I heard the number of them" (Revelation 9:16).

When this was recorded, two thousand years ago, nobody could even dream of a military army of two hundred million soldiers. However, today, it would be quite possible for some nations to join forces and field this number.

God is going to gather all of the armies of the earth together, they will come up against Israel and Jesus will come back with His army from heaven to defend His holy land and people. Jesus single handily will destroy all these Anti-Christ armies. In Nahum 2:4 above, we can see that this will be in a time and a day, when cars or chariots are raging in the streets or the highways. We live in a day when our freeways are jammed with cars bumper to bumper, day and night running to and fro. Governments all over the world are trying to deal with car congestion, fossil fuel cars and they are trying to find solutions via other forms of transport for this problem, another sign that we are living in the days of the soon return of Christ.

Salt of the Earth

Jesus said that we are the salt of the earth, salt preserves! The ancient mariners would put their meat in barrels of salt water to preserve it on their long journeys. If the salt was removed, the meat would soon go rotten. When the church, which is the restraining force, the preservative of the earth, departs, the earth will go bad or rotten. At The Rapture, when the church is caught away, Satan and his Anti-Christ will no longer be restrained. This is another reason why I believe strongly, in the pre tribulation Rapture of the Church.

CHAPTER SIXTEEN

JESUS WILL RETURN

The Bible tells us in the Book of Acts 1:11 that Jesus will come again. Jesus is coming back to establish a 1000 year reign of peace on the earth, known as the millennium. This will be after the seven year period of great holocausts referred to in the Bible as the tribulation (Matthew 24:29).

This seven year period will culminate or end with a great battle known as the Battle of Armageddon. At this battle, Jesus Christ and the returning armies of heaven will destroy the armies of the Antichrist and those that oppose Jesus Christ's kingdom.

The good news is that we do not have to be around for the seven years of tribulation.

> In the Book of 1 Thessalonians 4:16,17, it tells us, *"For the Lord Himself shall descend from heaven with a shout, with the voice of the archangel, and with the trump of God: and the dead in Christ shall rise first:*

Then we which are alive and remain shall be caught up together with them in the clouds, to meet the Lord in the air: and so shall we ever be with the Lord."

This *'catching up'* or *'harpazo'* as it is referred to in the Greek, means to seize, catch up, snatch away or "I seize, snatch, obtained by robbery." The Word *'Rapture'* does not appear in the Bible, but the dictionary meaning of the word rapture is, to be caught up with great joy. So because of these meanings the 'catching away of the church' has become commonly known as 'The Rapture' In 1 Thessalonians 5:9 it tells us that God has not appointed His children to wrath, but to obtain salvation by our Lord Jesus Christ.

In Old Testament teachings, especially the book of Daniel, the last seven year period is called Daniel's Seventieth Week. It is a period made up of two halves, both three and a half years long. Jesus calls this time, the time of great tribulation, it will be worse than any other time in human history. It is a time of God's great judgement on planet earth for all of the sins, atrocities and evil that has been carried out down through the centuries against God and mankind.

It will literally be God pouring out His judgement on the earth and all of the powers of wickedness and evil on this planet. God does not want His children to go through this extremely terrible time.

Before the world enters this last seven year period, which in the Book of Matthew Chapter 24, are described as terrible years of wars, famines, earthquakes, pestilences etc., Jesus will come in the clouds of the air and catch His church, that is those who are born again, His followers, away.

> Luke 21:36, *"Watch ye therefore, and pray always, that ye may be accounted worthy to escape all these things that shall come to pass, and to stand before the Son of man."*

The word here 'escape' in the Greek breakdown, means to vanish away from, to flee out of.

Jesus has promised that He will come back at His second coming to usher in His one thousand year millennial reign. I had a good friend by the name of Marvin Ford. He had died, and at that time, his Pastor (David Wilkinson) went into his hospital room, prayed for him and he was raised from the dead. Marvin shared with me, that during his time in heaven, he met Jesus who told him his ministry was not finished and he would have to go back to finish his course!

Jesus gave him an assignment to inform people about His second coming that would follow the time of great tribulation. He told Marvin that before He comes with His church at the second coming, He is coming for His church at the rapture. But before He comes for His church, He is coming to His church in great healing signs, power and glory.

The church before this seven years of great tribulation, will vanish away from the earth. And like Jesus was in the Book of Acts 1: 9 &10, the born again believers will be caught up to heaven, where we will live for seven years, until we return with our Lord Jesus Christ to enter into His millennial reign on this earth.

In the book of 1 Thessalonians 5:1-3 Paul writes,

> *"But of the times and the seasons, brethren, you have no need that I write unto you. For yourselves know perfectly that the day of the Lord so cometh as a thief in the night. For when they shall say, Peace and safety; then sudden destruction cometh upon them, as travail upon a woman with child; and they shall not escape."*

Jesus speaks about a time, that he refers to as the beginning of sorrows.

Matthew 24:8 tells us, *"All these are the beginning of sorrows."*

The beginning of sorrows is likened through the word of God, as a woman in travail about to give birth. It is birth pains! The closer the woman gets to the hour of birth, the more intense the pains and the closer the contractions.

I believe that right now we are in a time of the beginning of sorrows, at the end of the dispensation of 'Grace'. The world is about to enter the time of 'Tribulation'. At the end of this time, Jesus will fulfil His word and He will return to take control of the earth as Lord of Lords and King of Kings.

Be Rapture Ready

Matthew 24:44 tells us, *"Therefore, be ye also ready, for in such an hour as ye think not the Son of man cometh."*

1 Corinthians 15:51&52 also speaks of this mystery (rapture):

> *"Behold, I shew you a mystery; We shall not all sleep, but we shall all be changed, In a moment, in the twinkling of an eye, at the last trump: for the trumpet shall sound, and the dead shall be raised incorruptible, and we shall be changed."*

Jesus promised us in the Book of John 14 that He would come back for us, in verses 1-3: *"Let not your heart be troubled: ye believe in God, believe also in Me. In My Father's house are many mansions: if it were not so, I would have told you. I go to prepare a place for you. And if I go and prepare a place for you, I will come again and receive you unto Myself; that where I am there ye may be also."*

We can see from the current uncertain times we are living in, that the days before the return of our Lord Jesus Christ are drawing to a close. We are very close to the return of our Lord Jesus Christ.

> Romans 8:21-22 tells us, *"Because creation itself also shall be delivered from the bondage of corruption into the glorious liberty of the children of God. For we know that the whole creation groaneth and travaileth in pain together until now."*

As we draw closer to the end of the beginning of sorrows and the start of the great tribulation, the trials, tribulations, pandemics, earthquakes, natural disasters, sicknesses, mental health issues, wars and different types of wars causing heartache, famine and loss etc., will increase in magnitude and severity. They will get closer and closer together, affecting the entire earth. Great fear will be released upon the nations and the hearts and minds of people. Political leaders and governments will be in a quandary, mentally at a loss, not knowing what to do.

Recently a Pastor friend of mine asked me about the Return of Christ and the Rapture of the Church and what we can do to be ready when Jesus returns. Remember, Jesus told us to be like the five wise virgins that had oil in their lamps so that they could go into the safe place with Him (this I believe refers to the rapture).

> Matthew 25:6-10 says, *"At midnight the cry rang out: 'Here's the bridegroom! Come out to meet him!' Then all the virgins woke up and trimmed their lamps. The foolish ones said to the wise, 'Give us some of your oil; our lamps are going out.' "'No,' they replied, 'there may not be enough for both us and you. Instead, go to those who sell oil and buy some for yourselves.' "But while they were on their way to buy the oil, the bridegroom arrived. The virgins who were ready went in with him to the wedding banquet. And the door was shut."*

The Rapture is a Type of the Ark

Here is what I shared with my friend. The rapture is a type of ark. In the Old Testament, God instructed Noah to build an ark. This Ark was to save mankind and the animals from the impending judgement of God. This judgement was coming because of the rampant spread of wickedness, sin and evil deeds that people were doing before God and to each other.

Jesus said, *"As in the days of Noah, so shall it be in the days before I return."*

Noah was a preacher of righteousness and he warned people that God's judgement was coming and they should repent and prepare for it. There was a chance, an open door in the ark for people to enter before judgement fell. God gave everyone a chance to be saved.

Right now, God is giving everybody a chance to repent and be saved, ready to go in the rapture or the catching away of the church before God's judgement falls. I see the preparation time and building of the ark, as a type of beginning of sorrows that Jesus spoke of, before the judgement falls and a new day is born.

During this time, we must return to our first love. Make sure we are doing our best to win souls and prepare them for the rapture and the second coming of the Lord.

As previously stated in Luke 21:36, Jesus instructs us to watch and pray. We are to discern the times and seasons and not be ignorant or have our heads buried in the sand. We only have to look around, watch the news and we can see what is going on. We are then to pray, lifting up our eyes and staying in fellowship with our Lord Jesus and God our Father, through prayer.

As the Holy Spirit convicts and leads, we are to forsake and repent of our sins. We can do this regularly by taking communion with the Lord. Please read the last chapter on communion, in this book.

Kenneth Hagin would say, "Faith begins where the will of God is known." We must know that it is God's will to deliver us and keep us safe from the time of His great judgement and the wrath to come.

Raptured by Faith

Every promise of God is received into our lives by faith. Through faith, we receive the blessings of the Lord. Salvation is received by grace through faith. It is a gift of God. We receive healing by faith in the work of the grace of our Lord Jesus Christ at the cross. I believe, we receive salvation, healing, baptism of the Spirit, financial breakthrough and every other gift from God by faith. In the same way, we get raptured by faith. We must believe in it to participate in it! As Jesus said, "We watch and stay in prayer that we be accounted worthy to escape away from all that is coming on the earth and to stand before the Son of Man." Remember, Abraham's faith was accounted to him as righteousness.

> Hebrews 11:5-6 says, *"By faith Enoch was taken from this life, so that he did not experience death: "He could not be found, because God had taken him*

> away." For before he was taken, he had this testimony that he pleased God. And without faith, it is impossible to please God, because anyone who comes to him must believe that he is and that he is a rewarder of those who diligently seek him."

Here we can see Enoch was raptured by faith because he pleased God. Let's do those things that are pleasing to God. Let us love God with all of our heart and love each other as we love ourselves.

Let's be vigilant and discerning in these times, as Jesus said, "Watching and praying." Let's continue to grow through life by constantly staying in communion with God, keeping our lamps filled with the Holy Spirit oil and the Word of God, waiting for that great day when Jesus comes to catch us away.

Faith pleases God, so let us have faith in all the promises of God. God is a rewarder of those who diligently seek Him. God wants to deliver you and your family from the judgement and the great tribulation to come, just like He delivered Noah and his family, from the judgement at that time.

Keep Your Eyes Open

> Hebrews 9:28 says, *"So Christ was once offered to bear the sins of many; and unto them that look for Him shall He appear the second time without sin unto salvation."*

Revelation 22:20: *"He which testifieth these things saith, 'Surely I come quickly. Amen.' Even so, come, Lord Jesus."*

Chapter Seventeen

TIMELINES

Often people ask me questions concerning timelines and when do I think The Rapture is going to happen? These were the same questions that were asked of Jesus. We find this in Matthew 24:3,

> *"And as he sat upon the mount of Olives, the disciples came unto him privately, saying, Tell us, when shall these things be? and what shall be the sign of thy coming, and of the end of the world?"*

We see three basic questions here:
1. When shall these things be?
2. What shall be the sign of Your coming?
3. When shall be the end of the age?

These questions by the disciples were in response to a statement that Jesus had made concerning the temple in Jerusalem.

"And Jesus went out, and departed from the temple: and his disciples came to him for to shew him the buildings of the temple. And Jesus said unto them, See ye not all these things? verily I say unto you, There shall not be left here one stone upon another, that shall not be thrown down" (Matthew 24:1-2).

Jesus then proceeds to teach them and to give them revelation in Matthew 24 & 25, answers to the questions they had just asked.

Now we know from history, that after Jesus was crucified and raised from the dead, then raptured up into heaven, at approximately 30-34 AD. We know that the Jewish temple was destroyed in 70 AD. As a result of the first Jewish revolt the Roman military blockaded and sieged Jerusalem. The Romans destroyed much of the city and the second temple. At that time approximately one million Jews were killed and most of the survivors were sold into slavery or scattered into the nations. There was a very small number that remained in the land throughout this dispersion. In 135 AD, the Jews were completely barred from Jerusalem for several centuries and the city of Jerusalem was given a different name.

Over the next nineteen centuries, the religious Jews prayed and cried out to God for restoration of their homeland and to be returned to their beloved, Jerusalem.

31st October 1917
The British and ANZAC military forces capture Beersheba from the Turks and Germans, which paves the way for the

British conquest of Palestine. On the same day the British Cabinet decides to pave the way for the creation of a Jewish homeland in Palestine. The decision is published by Foreign Secretary Arthur Balfour two days later in what became known as The Balfour Declaration.

9th December 1917
The British and ANZAC forces conquer Jerusalem, bringing an end to 400 years of Ottoman Turkish rule. Two days later, on the eve of the Feast of Chanukkah, the British General Allenby ceremonially enters Jerusalem, declaring British rule over Palestine.

14th May 1948
The last High Commissioner, Sir Alan Cunningham, leaves Palestine and the British Mandate ends. At 4pm David Ben Gurion, the recognised leader of the Jewish people, declares the existence of the sovereign State of Israel, according to UN Resolution 181.

7th June 1967
Israel captured the old city of Jerusalem.

Then in the **6th December 2017**, the then President Donald Trump moved the American embassy to Jerusalem and recognised it as the capital of Israel. Declaring our greatest hope is for peace.

> *"Now learn a parable of the fig tree; When his branch is yet tender, and puts forth leaves, ye know that summer is near:"* (Matthew 24:32).

God had prophesied in His Word that because His people had forsaken and rejected Him and His ways that He would reject them. Through the Old Testament, we see prophecies that the second temple would be destroyed and the people of Israel scattered through the nations until the time of the end.

> *"Therefore you shall stumble in the day; The prophet also shall stumble with you in the night; And I will destroy your mother. My people are destroyed for lack of knowledge. Because you have rejected knowledge, I also will reject you from being priest for Me; Because you have forgotten the law of your God, I also will forget your children. "The more they increased, the more they sinned against Me; I will change their glory into shame"* (Hosea 4:5-7 NKJV).

Like some Christians today, Israel backslid away from God. Hosea 4:16a says, *"For Israel slides back as a backsliding heifer:"*

God gave a time to this backsliding, we know that a thousand years is like a day to God and a day is a thousand years. From our timeline above, we know that Israel was scattered for nineteen centuries, until **1948** when the nation was reborn in a day.

> *"I will go and return to my place, till they acknowledge their offence, and seek my face: in their affliction they will seek me early. Come, and let us return unto the Lord: for he hath torn, and he will heal us;*

he hath smitten, and he will bind us up. After two days will he revive us: in the third day he will raise us up, and we shall live in his sight. Then shall we know, if we follow on to know the Lord: his going forth is prepared as the morning; and he shall come unto us as the rain, as the latter and former rain unto the earth" (Hosea 5:15-6:3).

We can see in the above verse, where God allotted two days or two thousand years for the Jews to be in exile. This finished in 1948 and marked the beginning of the last generation of time before the fulfilment of all things. Jesus taught this in answer to the disciples' questions, *"When shall these things be?"*

"So likewise ye, when ye shall see all these things, know that it is near, even at the doors. Verily I say unto you, this generation shall not pass, till all these things be fulfilled. Heaven and earth shall pass away, but my words shall not pass away" (Matthew 24:33-35).

In Psalm 90, we see the length of a generation and a beautiful picture of The Rapture and then the impending Tribulation, which is the wrath of God poured out on the earth.

"The days of our years are threescore years and ten; and if by reason of strength they be fourscore years, yet is their strength labour and sorrow; for it is soon cut off, and we fly away. Who knows the power of

thine anger? even according to thy fear, so is thy wrath. So teach us to number our days, that we may apply our hearts unto wisdom"* (Psalm 90:10-12).

Notice, that the seventy to eighty years and then *"we fly away"*.

"But of that day and hour knows no man, no, not the angels of heaven, but my Father only. But as the days of Noah were, so shall also the coming of the Son of man be" (Matthew 24:36-37).

No one knows the day nor the hour of The Rapture of the church, but we can know the approximate season and time, firstly from God's timelines and secondly from signs of the times. Notice Jesus said, *"As it was in the days of Noah."* Noah didn't know the day that God would shut the door of the Ark, however He knew the approximate time. God had told Noah, that His Spirit would not always strive with man (Genesis 6:3), but his days would be a hundred and twenty years. So Noah knew that from when he began to build the Ark, God's judgement would fall in the one hundredth and twentieth year. It is interesting to note that the year 2017, when Jerusalem was recognized again, as the capital of Israel, it was 120 years of Super Jubilees.

From 1948, if we add seventy years we get the year 2018. If we add 80, we get the year 2028. From these timelines, you can see we are fast approaching The Rapture of the Church and the second coming of the Lord Jesus Christ. We may not know the exact day or hour, but we are in a thin slither of time, between the second day, as spoken of in Hosea, and third day, which is the millennial reign of Christ. God has declared revival for this time and greater glory for the church!

> *"And I will shake all nations, and the desire of all nations shall come: and I will fill this house with glory, says the Lord of hosts. The silver is mine, and the gold is mine, says the Lord of hosts. The glory of this latter house shall be greater than of the former, says the Lord of hosts: and in this place will I give peace, says the Lord of hosts"* (Haggai 2:7-9).

Jesus spoke of earthquakes, in every quadrant of the earth at the same time. This is happening in our world right now, as earthquake and volcanic activity is dramatically on the increase. Jesus also spoke of pestilences. The coronavirus has shaken all the nations of the earth and caused great fear. Great fear everywhere is another sign that the end is near. Jesus spoke of The Rapture in Matthew 24:40-42.

> *"Then shall two be in the field; the one shall be taken, and the other left. Two women shall be grinding at the mill; the one shall be taken, and the other left. Watch therefore: for ye know not what hour your Lord doth come"* (Matthew 24:40-42).

> *"Therefore be you also ready: for in such an hour as you think not the Son of man comes"* (Matthew 24:44).

Our Lord Jesus taught that in the last days, there would be great deception in the earth and that His believers were to be aware and careful of this. We are to stay in the Word and keep our eyes on Jesus.

> Jesus also said, *"As in the days of Lot, so shall it be in the days of the coming of the Son of Man"* (Luke 17:28 & 30).

The Rapture, Part of Abraham's Blessings

God delivered Lot, His wife and daughters from Sodom and Gomorrah, before His judgement fell on these two cities. He did this, because of His promise to Abraham. God will deliver us at the Rapture, before He pours out His judgement on earth, due to it's rebellion to His ways, because of His promise to Abraham.

> *"And if you be Christ's, then are you Abraham's seed, and heirs according to the promise"* (Galatians 3:29).

We are now living in days, when same sex marriage is approved and accepted by the majority of nations and governments in the earth. In the days of Lot, in the cities of Sodom and Gomorrah, same sex partnership was very common and accepted in these cities as the norm. People may not realize this, but this contravenes God's original plan and purpose, according to the Bible, His Holy Word. So Jesus is describing a time, when history would repeat itself. Today, same-sex partnership, along with fornication, multiple sex partners and the break down of the family unit, have become accepted as a normal and natural lifestyle. This is a far cry from what God originally intended for His creation. The Lord Jesus gives us many insights and warnings as to when God's judgement will fall, and how we can identify those days and times. All have sinned and fallen short of God's glory and His original plans and purposes for all people of all nations. There is none righteous, no not one. Hell was made for the devil and his angels. Hell was not made for people. God must judge the earth for its sins and wrong doings and set things that have gone out of whack with His original plans, back into correct alignment again. When God brings judgement, it is ultimately for blessing and life. Right now every one of us has an opportunity to find Jesus and receive Him as our Lord and Saviour, knowing that He paid the price for our sins, in order that we might have forgiveness and eternal life through Him.

Jesus also said that in these days, the love of many will grow cold, but he that endures to the end would be saved. He said that His Gospel of the Kingdom would be preached in all the world for a witness unto every nation and then the end shall come. He then referred to the prophecies of Daniel the prophet, and the coming of the Anti-Christ and his Kingdom. He referred to him as the 'abomination of desolation', satan's Anti-Christ, who during the last seven years, along with his people (that is the nations and people that have entered into an alliance with Him) will enter into a peace treaty with Israel. In the middle of these seven years, he will break this peace treaty and proclaim himself as God. The False Prophet, that backs him, will force everyone to be sealed with the number of the Anti-Christ, which is 666. No one will be able to buy or sell without this number. And refusing to worship the Anti-Christ and take this number, will result in the death for those individuals. Thank God for the Rapture that happens before this system is implemented.

People ask me, what does this mean? In my opinion, if we look at our current world and what is transpiring, many governments are trying to put in place a system that prevents unvaccinated people from the Covid virus and it's variants, from participating in many activities such as sport, restaurants, theatre, bars, festivals, movies and many other of life's activities that we take for granted and have become a normal part of modern day living. This would have been unheard of just a couple of years ago. I ask the question, where is all this leading to? As God's people, we do not have to fear the Anti-Christ system or the 666 mark. We will be caught up, by Jesus into glory before it begins. But with the advances in technology, we can see in our generation, how, an Anti-Christ backed by a One World Government could implement this. The technology and advances in science and computing, are allowing now for one such system. This system could be hacked or taken over, to take advantage of and control the populations of the earth. This is prophesied in God's word.

> *"And he deceives those who dwell on the earth by those signs which he was granted to do in the sight of the beast, telling those who dwell on the earth to make an image to the beast who was wounded by the sword and lived. He was granted power to give breath to the image of the beast, that the image of the beast should both speak and cause as many as would not worship the image of the beast to be killed. He*

causes all, both small and great, rich and poor, free and slave, to receive a mark on their right hand or on their foreheads, and that no one may buy or sell except one who has the mark or the name of the beast, or the number of his name. Here is wisdom. Let him who has understanding calculate the number of the beast, for it is the number of a man: His number is 666" (Revelation 13:14-18 NKJV).

Knowledge Shall Increase

People today are requiring easier methods of banking, data keeping, doing business and commerce. We are living in a fast-paced, technological breakthrough society. Knowledge and information are increasing at an exponential rate. This is an end-time sign.

"But you, Daniel, shut up the words, and seal the book until the time of the end; many shall run to and fro, and knowledge shall increase" (Daniel 12:4).

Governments are looking at digital identity, digital passports, and vaccine certificates to implement into their systems, including travel, international borders, commerce and business. The private sector is in a race to bring better, more convenient and faster technology to implement all of this. These technological advancements are great, but not if they take away our God-given freedoms. Digital surveillance is increasing to a point, where your whereabouts is known at all times.

Medical technology is advancing to where a human's DNA can be cut and a new code can be edited in. If you look up 'CRISPRgene editing' on Wikipedia, you can read about how this process works. It is a genetic engineering technique in molecular biology, by which the genomes of living organisms may be modified. It is based on a simplified version of the bacterial CRISPR-Cas9 antiviral defence system. By delivering the Cas9nuclease complex with a synthetic guide RNA (gRNA) into a cell, the cells' genomes can be cut at a desired location, allowing existing genes to be removed and or new ones added in living organisms. We know that a number of the new vaccines are using mRNA technology. The 'M' stands for messenger. Now I'm not a scientist, but these are new messages that can be delivered into our cells.

Messenger RNA is a single strand of RNA molecule that is complimentary to one of the DNA strands of a gene. It moves into sytoplasm where proteins are made. During protein synthesis, in an organelle cell, a ribosome moves along the mRNA, reads base sequence, and uses the genetic code to translate each three-base triplet, or codon, into its corresponding amino acid.

This modern technology; as brilliant as it is, could be opening a Pandora's box. Scientific and innovation companies are working on patches, which I believe could be described as QR-codes under the skin. It is not a big stretch of the mind to see a day in the not too distant future, when subcutaneous records of banking, ID and medical are all under and contained in a person's hand. A future Anti-Christ and beast system, could then easily force his 666 business/e-commerce system to be added to a person's record. Whereby without the 666, a person could not buy or sell, or operate in any way in normal life. A person would be basically cut off and shut out of society if they didn't comply.

I am not saying that any of the companies involved in inventing and bringing this technology into our world, or society and economy are part of the beast system. However, I believe, that because this breakthrough technology is being invented and trialled in people, it is another sign that we are in the end times and living in the last days.

The Anti-Christ along with his False Prophet, will just take full advantage of the technology of the day to implement his government and trading systems. It is interesting to note, that a class of oxidative enzymes that produce the bioluminescence that will be used under the skin to be read by a special light or app in a smart phone is called "Luciferase". This word comes from the Latin word 'Lucifer'. Lucifer was an angel who rebelled against God and became the devil after he fell and he will give his power to the Anti-Christ, during the time of The Great Tribulation.

An article in MIT news on December 18th 2019, was about how in the future medical information could be stored under a person's skin's surface. This would be possible by using a special dye (Luciferase could be that dye). This dye would be invisible to the eye and could enable "on-patient storage of vaccination history". This would be in the form of a digital record under the skin.

So then this mark could then be scanned for human compliance. Ultimately, ID and banking records could be added and we would have a system that could be placed in a person's hand, just like the Bible describes in the book of Revelation 13:16-18. Companies today are even creating these types of systems that measure brain waves, body activity data and body heat and will reward people with cryptocurrency. If this is implemented it will move the world closer to a cashless economy. Mircrosoft has even applied for a patent and the number of the patent is W2020 060606. Governments have also brought into law surveillance and tracking systems. Google 'H. R. 6666' and you will find information about this act of American congress. It provides grants related to activities such as contact tracing, through mobile health units and as necessary, at individuals' residences and for other purposes and is related to the 2003 biological, chemical and radiological weapons counter measures, Research Act (s.666). I find this information and number patterns absolutely fascinating. You yourself can do a deeper dive and research into this and the advances of this science and technology which will ultimately include banking.

As stated, I am not saying that any of these companies or governments are part of the Anti-Christ government or system. I just believe that because we are living in the last days we are seeing everything come together and put into place that after The Rapture of the Church, when the Anti-Christ comes into power, everything he needs to implement his systems would have been invented and lots of them will be in every day use. He will just then forcibly add his 666 halfway into his reign and prevent anyone from doing any kind of commerce from that point in time, unless they take his mark and number. Failure to comply at that point in time, will result in the person's death.

We are definitely in the days of exponential knowledge, which is in itself an end-time sign. The populations of the earth have never moved around or travelled to and fro upon the earth, as they do today.

Another interesting scripture is in Obadiah 1:4.

"Though you exalt yourself as the eagle, and though you set your nest among the stars, from there I will bring you down," says the Lord" (Obadiah 1: 4).

We live in a time when NASA, along with private enterprise, and other governments of this world, are building space stations and planning to live in orbital homes around the earth, as well as future habitation on the moon, Mars and other planets. Never before in any time in history, has this been possible. Technology is advancing at such a rapid rate, that these things that were not possible are now possible and highly probable within our lifetime. God does not have a problem with technology, inventions or man going into space.

In fact, there is a scripture that says in the book of Proverbs 8:12, *"I wisdom dwell with prudence, and find out knowledge of witty inventions."*

God just wants us to live in His wisdom. He wants us to improve our way of life, community and living conditions for all mankind. God wants us to have optimum health. There is so much knowledge in God's word on how to achieve these things, so that all human beings can live a better lifestyle, enjoying life to the fullest. He just doesn't want us to do it without Him. God told us, pride comes before a fall in Proverbs 16:18,

"Pride goes before destruction, and an arrogant, superior spirit before a fall."

The love of money and pride was the reason that Lucifer fell. These attributes of his heart, changed his nature and he became Satan. God wants us to always put Him and His Kingdom first and humble ourselves under His mighty hand. When man (like Satan) gets the love of money, which is the root of ALL evil, then allows his heart to be full of pride, believing that he is a god, or ascending to be a god, this will lead his heart into many deceptions and evil ways, that will ultimately bring about his fall and destruction.

The more our world and society rejects God and pushes him out, making His word and His ways irrelevant, the faster God will intervene and bring about His judgement. Life without God, is no life at all. Because God is life, love and light. To reject God, and His ways, is ultimately a rejection of life, love and light.

> *"I call heaven and earth as witnesses today against you, that I have set before you life and death, blessing and cursing; therefore choose life, that both you and your descendants may live"* (Deuteronomy 30:19).

The Greatest Sign of the End of the Age

In my opinion, the greatest sign of the end of the age is The Rapture of the Church, when the Church departs at the great catching up.

"For the Lord Himself will descend from heaven with a shout, with the voice of an archangel, and with the trumpet of God. And the dead in Christ will rise first. Then we who are alive and remain shall be caught up together with them in the clouds to meet the Lord in the air. And thus we shall always be with the Lord" (1 Thessalonians 4:16-17).

After the church is taken out of the way, many that have heard about the Rapture will know that it has taken place. This will be a sign that Daniel's seventieth week is about to begin. During which time the Anti-Christ will seek to become world ruler.

The word caught up in the above verse is the Greek word "harphzo", and it means to seize, to catch up, to snatch away or take. A further study into this word reveals the meaning "to rescue from the danger of destruction!" It means, 'I seize, snatch or obtain by robbery'. Remember Jesus said, *"I come as a thief in the night"* (Revelation 16:15).

The book of Revelation is not very often read or taught. Yet in Revelation 1:3, Jesus promises us a blessing just for reading and hearing the words of this prophecy. I believe, God is revealing the book of Revelation to His children afresh, because we are at the time of the end. Many people are having visions and dreams on end times and The Rapture of the Church. This is because the Word declares, "At midnight a cry will go forth. Behold the Bridegroom comes". We are living in the midnight hour and I encourage every Believer to start to read the Book of Revelation verse by verse, from beginning to end. Remember, this is a Revelation of Jesus Christ declaring to us the things which must shortly come to pass.

As I have studied the word, I have found the Rapture from Genesis to Revelation. The first Rapture or catching up, was in Genesis 5:24, when Enoch was caught up to the presence of God. I have found The Rapture in Abraham's blessing. Galatians 3:29, *"If you be Christ's, then you are Abraham's seed and an heir of the blessing."* If we look at Genesis 19:27-29, we can see how God remembered Abraham and because of His covenant to Abraham, delivered Lot before His judgement fell.

> *"And Abraham went early in the morning to the place where he had stood before the Lord. Then he looked toward Sodom and Gomorrah, and toward all the land of the plain; and he saw, and behold, the smoke of the land which went up like the smoke of a furnace. And it came to pass, when God destroyed the cities of the plain, that God remembered Abraham, and sent Lot out of the midst of the overthrow, when He overthrew the cities in which Lot had dwelt"* (Genesis 19:27-29 NKJV).

The Jubilees

> *"And the Lord said, My spirit shall not always strive with man, for that he also is flesh: yet his days shall be an hundred and twenty years"* (Genesis 6:3).

TIMELINES

In this timeline below, I have tried to show you that there has been a hundred and twenty, fifty year Jubilees. The one hundred and twentieth super Jubilee occurred in 2017. There were other signs in the stars and their alignment that also occurred during this Jubilee year. This year was also the year that President Donald Trump moved the American embassy in Israel to Jerusalem, recognising Jerusalem as the capital of Israel. I believe that this is another significant event and marker that we are in the last years of the last days.

> *"After many days thou shalt be visited: in the latter years thou shalt come into the land that is brought back from the sword, and is gathered out of many people, against the mountains of Israel, which have been always waste: but it is brought forth out of the nations, and they shall dwell safely all of them"* (Ezekiel 38:8).

Let's not forget that God created the earth in six days, according to Genesis 1, on the seventh day He rested from all the work He had made. It has now been approximately six thousand years since the time of Adam and Eve (six days) and Jesus Christ will reign for a thousand years (one day). During the millennial reign of Christ the earth will be a rest and peace.

*Please see diagram on following page.

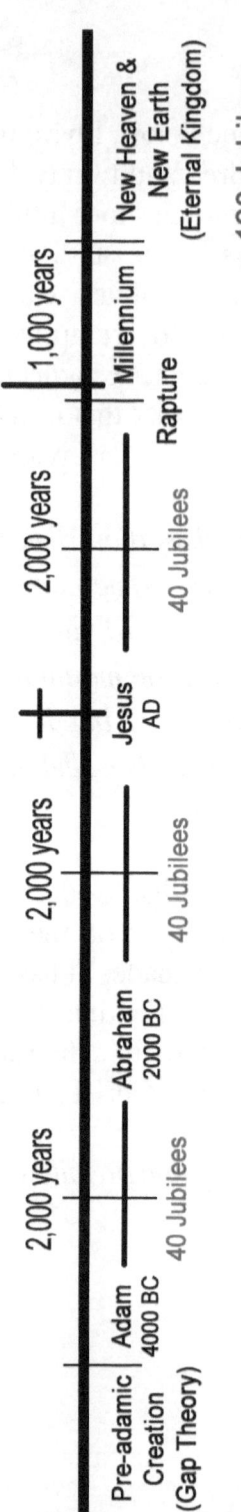

Daniel's Seventy Weeks

As referred to in different chapters of this book, I have laid out a timeline for Daniel's seventy weeks. This prophecy was given to Daniel by God and delivered by the angel Gabriel. This came about as a result of Daniel seeking the Lord as to the future of Jerusalem, Israel and the people of God. Daniel spent a time in fasting and prayer, asking and seeking God because at that time the temple was in ruins and the children of Israel had been carried off into Babylonian captivity. Daniel had spent time studying the prophecies of Jeremiah and other prophets and he understood, that by Jeremiah's prophecies that God would accomplish seventy years in the desolations of Jerusalem. Please refer to Daniel 9:1-27. He sought the Lord with tears, prayers and fasting to understand the prophecies of the prophets and the visions and dreams he was receiving from the Lord.

When Jesus was speaking about the end days and the sign of His coming, in Matthew 24 He referred to the prophet Daniel and his prophecies, including the seventieth week and the rise of the Anti-Christ in verse fifteen.

Please see diagram on following page.

THE OLD TESTAMENT'S MOST AMAZING PROPHECY

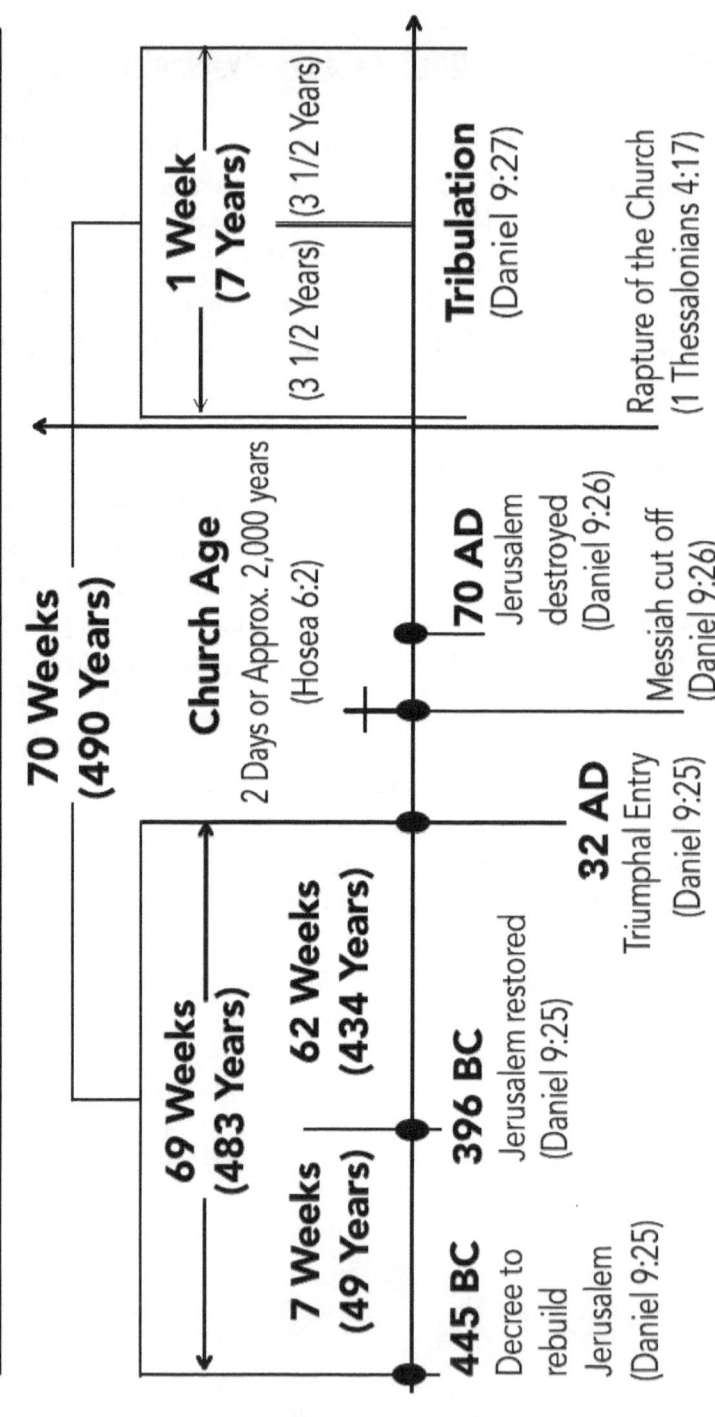

Signs in the Stars

23rd September 2017

In Genesis 1:14, God speaks about the stars, the sun and the moon, declaring them to be for signs and for seasons and for days.

> *"And God said, Let there be lights in the firmament of the heaven to divide the day from the night; and let them be for signs, and for seasons, and for days, and years: And let them be for lights in the firmament of the heaven to give light upon the earth: and it was so. And God made two great lights; the greater light to rule the day, and the lesser light to rule the night: he made the stars also"* (Genesis 1:14-16).

The word 'signs' here is the word 'oth' (original word nix). It comes from the word origin, 'avah', which means 'a sign'. This word means a sign, a banner, omen and witness. It is a sign or an omen promised by the prophets as pledges or certain predicted events. Over the course of history, God has showed many signs in the stars, sun and moon, prophetically to declare events. We can see in the bible, that at the time Christ was born a special star or astrological sign appeared over Bethlehem, declaring the birth of Christ. The Magi, or wise men, the Kings from the East, saw and understood, recognised the significance of this sign and followed it to the birth place of Christ.

In Luke 21:25 Jesus tells us, there will be signs in the sun, moon and stars.

THE RAPTURE OF THE CHURCH

"And there shall be signs in the sun, and in the moon, and in the stars; and upon the earth distress of nations, with perplexity; the sea and the waves roaring" (Luke 21:25).

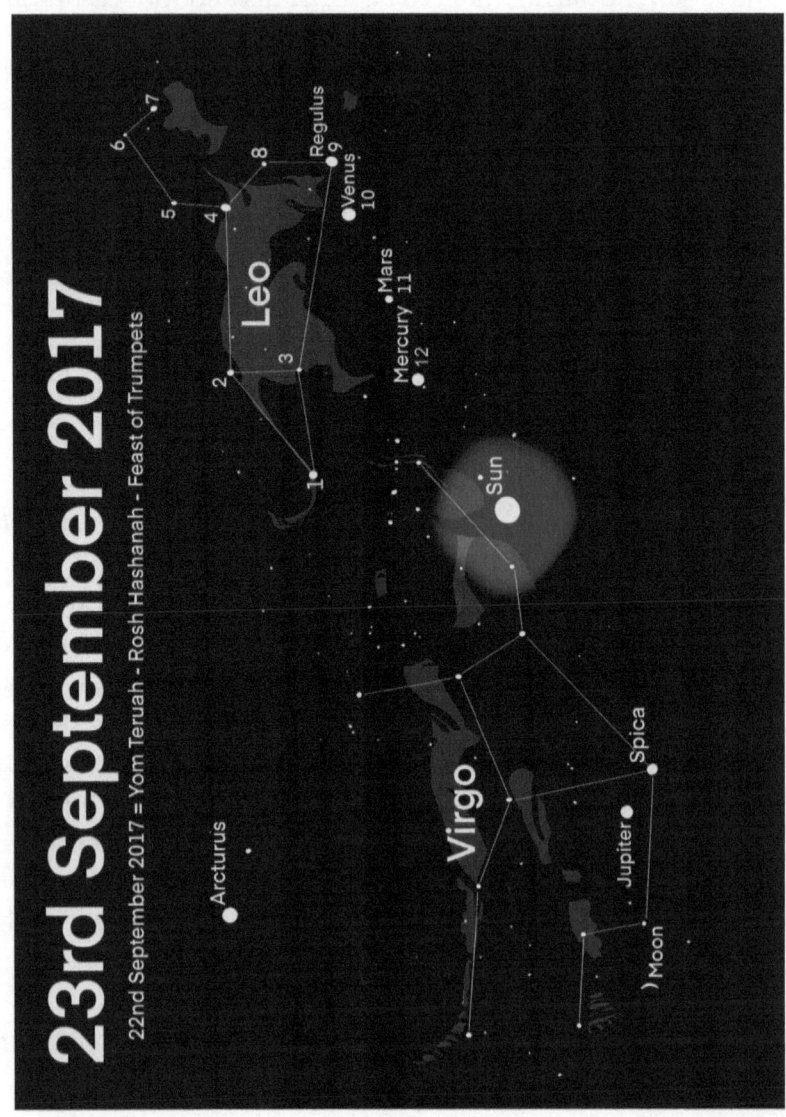

It is interesting to note that there are some bible scholars, prophets and astronomers that point out a star formation that appeared on the 23rd of September 2017, and was, as they say, "The Revelation 12 Sign".

> *"And there appeared a great wonder in heaven; a woman clothed with the sun, and the moon under her feet, and upon her head a crown of twelve stars: And she being with child cried, travailing in birth, and pained to be delivered. And there appeared another wonder in heaven; and behold a great red dragon, having seven heads and ten horns, and seven crowns upon his heads. And his tail drew the third part of the stars of heaven, and did cast them to the earth: and the dragon stood before the woman which was ready to be delivered, for to devour her child as soon as it was born. And she brought forth a man child, who was to rule all nations with a rod of iron: and her child was caught up unto God, and to his throne"* (Revelation 12:1-5).

Because this astrological sign appeared in 2017, the Super Jubilee year, when Jerusalem was recognized again as the capital of Israel, many end-time prophets believe it is another sign that points to The Rapture and the Great Tribulation.

Blood Moons

The blood moon prophecies were a series of prophecies by Christian preachers that related to a series of four full moons in 2014 and 2015. The prophecies stated that tetrad (a series of four consecutive lunar eclipses) that all coincided with Jewish feast days with six full moons in between and no intervening partial lunar eclipses. This was the beginning of end times, as known as, the Beginning of Sorrows. This began on the April 2014 lunar eclipse and this tetrad ended with the lunar eclipse on September 27-28 2015. Many modern day end time prophets believe this describes the scriptures in the book of Joel, and Acts 2:20 and Revelation 6:12.

I believe that as we draw closer to The Rapture, we are going to see more signs and wonders in the heavens, including activity in the sun and the moon. This will only increase during the time of tribulation, when the stars of heaven will fall to the ground, the sun and the moon darkened and the very powers of heaven shaken.

> *"Immediately after the tribulation of those days shall the sun be darkened, and the moon shall not give her light, and the stars shall fall from heaven, and the powers of the heavens shall be shaken: And then shall appear the sign of the Son of man in heaven: and then shall all the tribes of the earth mourn, and they shall see the Son of man coming in the clouds of heaven with power and great glory"* (Matthew 24:29-30).

Apophis

The bible speaks about great asteroids and stars that will fall from heaven to the earth during the time of the Great Tribulation. One such asteroid called 'Wormwood' in the book of Revelation 8:11, causes great destruction and many people die as a result.

> "The first angel sounded, and there followed hail and fire mingled with blood, and they were cast upon the earth: and the third part of trees was burnt up, and all green grass was burnt up. And the second angel sounded, and as it were a great mountain burning with fire was cast into the sea: and the third part of the sea became blood; And the third part of the creatures which were in the sea, and had life, died; and the third part of the ships were destroyed. And the third angel sounded, and there fell a great star from heaven, burning as it were a lamp, and it fell upon the third part of the rivers, and upon the fountains of waters; And the name of the star is called Wormwood: and the third part of the waters became wormwood; and many men died of the waters, because they were made bitter. And the fourth angel sounded, and the third part of the sun was smitten, and the third part of the moon, and the third part of the stars; so as the third part of them was darkened, and the day shone not for a third part of it, and the night likewise" (Revelation 8:7-12).

A huge asteroid by the name of Apophis will fly by earth on Friday, 13th April 2029. This asteroid which measures around 340 metres wide will pass within 31,000 km of the earth's surface. This is only one third of the distance from the earth to the moon. Some reports say it will pass through our stationary satellite belt. Let's not forget that often these huge rocks made of unknown substances, often are dragging with them many smaller rocks and meteors. Apophis, which means, "to slither; was often depicted in ancient art as a giant serpent that brings darkness and chaos", will be seen by over 2 billion people with the naked eye. Let's remember that Jesus said that the stars of heaven will fall to the earth. The above scripture reveals waters will be poisoned by what falls from heaven. It is quite possible, that Apophis could be one of these stars or asteroids that fall from heaven as spoken of by Jesus and other prophets in the Bible.

NASA is developing DART, a system to possibly try and change the direction of an asteroid from colliding with the earth, by crashing a spacecraft into it. One question that asteroid scientists have that is also vital for our planetary defence experts is the extent to which the sun's radiation nudges Apophis' orbit. This phenomenon is called the "Yarkovsky effect", that results from the temperature differences between the day and the night sides of the asteroids. If Apophis is Wormwood, then we will be getting raptured soon!

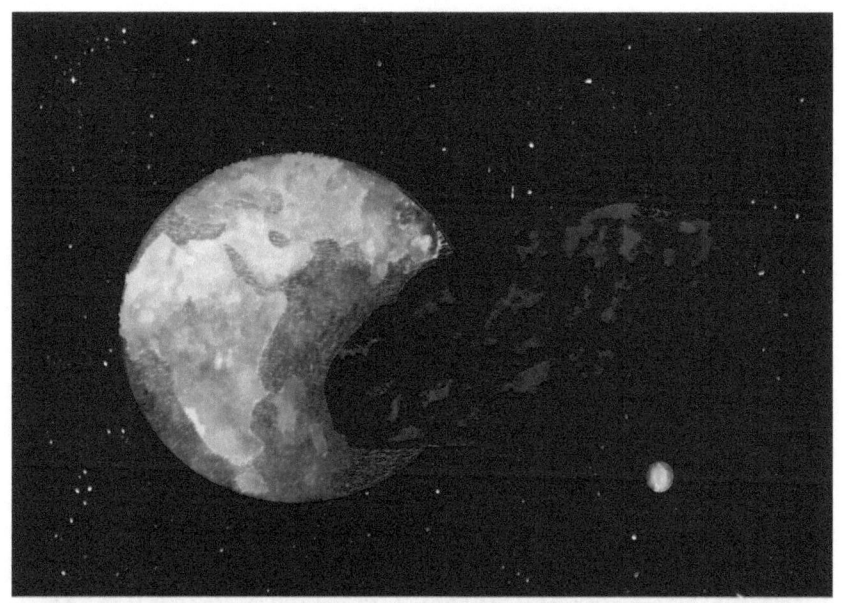

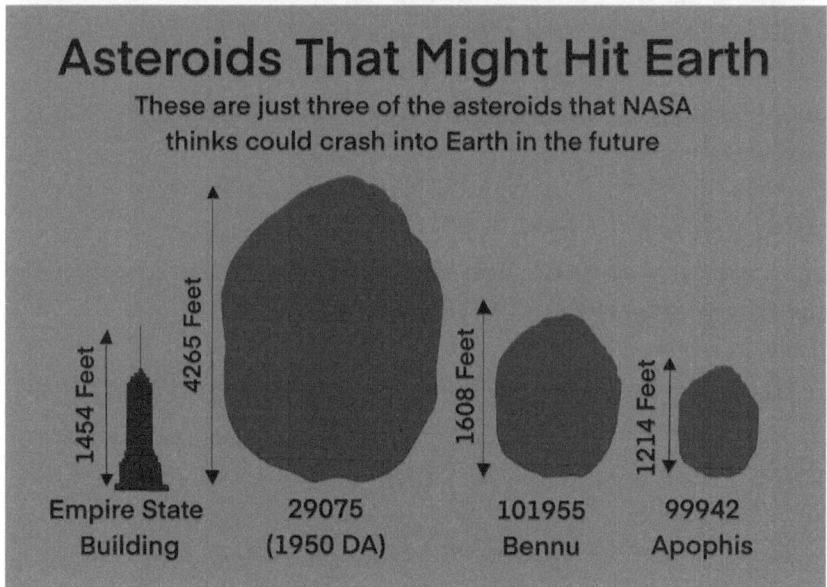

"For in the time of trouble he shall hide me in his pavilion: in the secret of his tabernacle shall he hide me; he shall set me up upon a rock" (Psalm 27:5).

PRAYER

Father I thank you that we can comfort one another because you haven't appointed your people to wrath, but to obtain salvation. Father we comfort one another with those words, that we haven't been appointed to the days of your wrath, to Israel's trouble, to Jacob's trouble, but we have been appointed to obtain salvation. And one of those blessings Lord, is to be translated, to be Raptured, to be caught up in the air with our Lord Jesus Christ, that we may ever be with Him.

I thank you Lord God for Your people. Thank you Lord that You encourage them, and You inspire them, to go out and proclaim the Gospel, but you keep their hearts and their minds in peace, knowing that they do not have to fear these things Lord, because You are their Saviour and, that You will catch them out of this place unto the Father God, before these days happen.

And Father, we thank You it is **Your Church** that preserves this earth, it is **Your Church** that restrains the evil one until we are taken out of the way. In Jesus Name. Amen.

If you have read this book but you have never received Jesus as your Lord and Saviour and would like to do so then go to the end of this book and pray the simple prayer I have included.

If you prayed that prayer and meant it, drop us a line and let us know so we can send you a letter and encourage you.

SOMEONE ASKED ME...

Shaun, what if you have got it all wrong? Well if I have got it all wrong, what have you got to lose by living your life right for God, departing from sin and looking for the coming of our Lord? NOTHING!

But maybe if I've got it right and this book helps set you free, inspiring you to live righteously for Jesus because that day is at hand and the time is very short. Then see you in the AIR!

God Bless You Real Good
Shaun

A final word from the author...

JESUS LOVES YOU

"The thief comes only to steal and kill and destroy; I have come that they may have life, and have it to the full." JOHN 10:10 (NIV)

You are very special. GOD LOVES YOU. He sent His son Jesus Christ who died for you and was raised from the dead. You are a somebody because you were created by God and He doesn't make nobodies.

Your are God's best, His dream, His idea.

"For I know the plans I have for you," declares the Lord, "plans to prosper you and not to harm you, plans to give you hope and a future. Then you will call upon me and come and pray to me, and I will listen to you. You will seek me and find me when you seek me with all your heart. I will be found by you, declares the Lord..." JEREMIAH 29:11-14 (NIV)

WHAT DOES GOD SAY?

ROMANS 3:23 "For all have sinned and fall short of the glory of God."

ROMANS 6:23 "The wages of sin is death, but the gift of God is eternal life in Christ Jesus our Lord."

JOHN 3:16 *"For God so loved the world that He gave His only begotten Son, that whosoever believes in Him should not perish but have everlasting life."*

ACTS 4:12 *"Nor is there salvation in any other name under heaven given among men by which we must be saved."*

TITUS 3:5 *"Not by works of righteousness which we have done, but according to His mercy He saved us…"*

1 JOHN 1:9 *"If we confess our sins He is faithful and just to forgive us our sins and cleanse us from all unrighteousness."*

2 CORINTHIANS 5:21 *"For He made Him who knew no sin to be sin for us, that we might become the righteousness of God in Him."*

ROMANS 10:9-10 *"That if you confess with your mouth the Lord Jesus and believe in your heart that God has raised Him from the dead, you will be saved. For with the heart one believes unto righteousness, and with the mouth confession is made unto salvation."*

Remember, Keep Your Eyes on Jesus!

Seek first the Kingdom of God and His righteousness. Keep your lamp filled (your life, heart and mind) by staying in the Word and prayer. Live life-ready, by being obedient, submitted and led by the Holy Spirit. Be quick to forgive and quick to repent if you make a mistake. Get up and get going for God again. Stay in fellowship with other Christians and your local church where possible. Know that God has not appointed you to the day of His wrath and judgement but to obtain salvation, through our Lord Jesus Christ. You will not only be life-ready but Rapture Ready!

SALVATION PRAYER

Here is a simple prayer you can pray in order to be born again:

Father, I come before you in the precious name of Jesus.
Lord, I have made mistakes in my life.
Father, I acknowledge that I have sinned.
I see in Your Word it says that Jesus died for my sins. Please forgive me of all of my sins and mistakes against you that I have committed, or any other person that I may have wronged.
I forgive all those who have sinned against me or wronged me in any way.
Father, I repent right now of my sins.
Father, I thank You that You sent Jesus, who came in the flesh and died for me, taking my sins on the cross, shedding His blood for me. Thank you, I am now clean from my sins, through the

shed blood of Jesus Christ. Thank you that on the third day You rose Jesus again from the dead. Jesus now sits at Your right hand in all power and glory, as King and Lord of all.

*Jesus, please come into my life, my heart, right now by the Person and power of the Holy Spirit, and make me born again.
Jesus, I receive You now as my Lord and my Saviour. Amen.*

Welcome to God's Family

If you prayed this simple prayer, you can know, according to God's Word that you are saved. You are now born again and have become a Christian, a follower of Christ. You must stand on His Word, not your feelings, emotions, or anything else. It is God's Word that guarantees your salvation.

Assurance of Salvation

*"And this is the record that God has given to us eternal life, and this life is in His Son. **HE THAT HAS THE SON HAS LIFE**, and he that has not the Son of God has not life. These things have I written unto you that believe on the name of the Son of God; **THAT YOU MAY KNOW** that ye have eternal life, and that ye may **BELIEVE ON THE NAME** of the Son of God."* (1 John 5: 11-13).

The Resurrection and the Life

Jesus said, "I am the Resurrection and the Life. He that believeth in Me, though he were dead, yet shall he live. And whosoever liveth and believeth in Me shall never die." (John 11:25-26).

Isn't that wonderful? I encourage all who read this to embrace this truth from the Word of God. Today, receive Jesus Christ as your personal Lord and Saviour. Your name will then be found in the Lord's Book of Life. (Revelation 3:5, 20:15 & Luke 10:20).

If you prayed that prayer and meant it, drop us a line and let us know so we can send you a letter and encourage you.

Jesus said in Luke 4:18-19, *"The Spirit of the Lord is upon me, because he hath anointed me to preach the gospel to the poor; he hath sent me to heal the brokenhearted, to preach deliverance to the captives, and recovering of sight to the blind, to set at liberty them that are bruised. To preach the acceptable year of the Lord."*

Jesus ushered in the Age of Grace, the time of the church. He never finished the scripture in Isaiah 61:2, *"To proclaim the acceptable year of the Lord, and the day of vengeance of our God; to comfort all that mourn."*

I believe it is midnight and it is now our responsibility to warn people that the day of vengeance of our God is fast approaching. Let's get our lives right and live for Jesus! All the church will be comforted at The Rapture when we get to see our families again that died in Christ and we are caught up with them together to be with Jesus forever!

Revelation 3:10

"Because thou hast kept the word of my patience, I also will keep thee from the hour of temptation (trial, testing, calamity, affliction) *which shall come upon all the world, to try them that dwell upon the earth."*

Footnotes

The following is a list of resources and sources, read and studied in the preparation of this book. Plus, further thank-yous and acknowledgements to individuals who have had an impact on my life. Their thoughts, prayers and inspiration (some of which I have included in this work) have helped mould me, enlighten my thinking and inspired me to grow and touch this world for Christ.

King James Bible
Amplified Bible. Jointly published by Zondervan and The Lockman Foundation.
NIV Bible. Published by Zondervan in the United States and Hodder & Stoughton in the UK.
New King James Version by Thomas Nelson.
Strong's Concordance. Published by Thomas Nelson Publishers.
Dake Annotated Reference Bible. Published by Dake's Publishing Inc.
Bible Hub. biblehub.com
Google Dictionary
'The Ancient Jewish Wedding' by Jamie Lash.
Reference for definition of 'marriage': https://www.merriam-webster.com/dictionary/marriage - Page 162-163.
 The Lion Handbook to the Bible (5th Edition) by Pat Alexander, David Alexander, published by Lion Hudson Publishing.
The Pre-Tribulation Rapture of the Church (A Joyful Looking for His Appearing) by Hilton Sutton, published by Harrison House.
N. B. page 113, page 254 - As stated, I am not saying that any of these companies or governments are part of the Anti-Christ government or system. I just believe that because we are living in the last days we are seeing everything come together and put into place that after The Rapture of the Church, when the Anti-Christ comes into power, everything he needs to implement his systems would have been invented and lots of them will be in every day use. He will just then forcibly add his 666 half way into his reign.

ABOUT THE AUTHOR

Dr Shaun Marler is the Senior Pastor and co-founder with his wife Kerrie of World Harvest Ministries, an international organisation based in Queensland, Australia, World Harvest Ministries is committed to carrying out the Great Commission of Jesus our Lord. Taking the healing word to the nations and feeding the hungry, visiting prisoners, clothing the naked, visiting the widows and orphans in their affliction, and preaching the Good News to the poor.

World Harvest Ministries currently has programs in Australia, Africa and India, where the poor and destitute are given free medical treatment, orphan homes where children are fed, accommodated and educated, a ministry to widows who have been abandoned by society and a program to feed people with leprosy.

A portion of the proceeds of the sale of this book goes towards this valuable work, which is making a huge difference in the lives of others!

Also by Dr. Shaun Marler

Life Changing Principles For Victorious Living.
Forewords by noted authors, Jerry Savelle, Col Stringer and Jim Kilbler. Life Changing Principles for Victorious Living is a must read! You will find keys to unlock your life in Christ.

Praise Power
Foreword by Dr Reg Klimionok
Everything in your life is subject to change. God's will for your life is that it changes for the better. How do you get there? Through praise in the Word, because praise is the verbal expression of Faith and Faith is the language of Heaven.

Divine Healing 101
Foreword by Joshua Mills
This is a how-to book with examples, teachings and personal testimonies, that prove it is God's will that you not only be healed, but walk in divine health, all the days of your life.

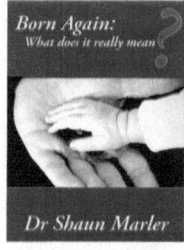

Born Again; What does it really mean?
This mini book is a must have! You will learn how you can accept Jesus Christ as Saviour and what it really means to be born again. Discover how you can enjoy all the blessings will now belong to you!

These books and other titles are available on Amazon as well as other online bookstores around the world!

Partnership

Help Pastor Shaun to help others, by becoming a Harvest partner in this great work of spreading the gospel and loving others.

Please email general@whm.org.au and become a World Harvest partner today!

For other information and a complete list of products, or to find out how you can partner with the ministry of Dr Shaun Marler and World Harvest Ministries, contact:

P.O. Box 90, Bald Hills, 4036
Queensland, Australia
Phone: +61 7 3261 4555
(9am – 4:30pm EST Aust)

Web: whm.org.au
Email: general@whm.org.au

Facebook: www.facebook.com/worldharvestmin
Facebook: www.facebook.com/ShaunMarlerWHM
Twitter: twitter.com/world_harvest
Youtube: youtube.com/worldharvestlife
Instagram: @i_harvest

www.ingramcontent.com/pod-product-compliance
Lightning Source LLC
Chambersburg PA
CBHW031237290426
44109CB00012B/339